Emily Post
on
Invitations and Letters

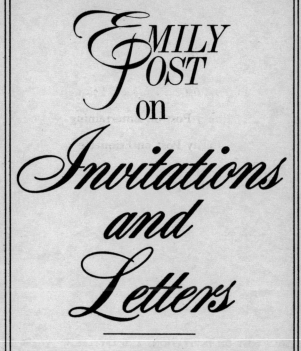

EMILY POST on Invitations and Letters

Elizabeth L. Post

PERENNIAL LIBRARY

Harper & Row, Publishers, New York
Grand Rapids, Philadelphia, St. Louis, San Francisco
London, Singapore, Sydney, Tokyo, Toronto

FIRST EDITION

Designed by Kim Llewellyn

ISBN 0-06-274005-9

Contents

Introduction

While it is true that I would be glad to receive a note scribbled on the back of a grocery list from old friends who have been incommunicado for years, and while some of my most cherished letters are pages of news, confidences, and insights dashed off on paper torn from a spiral notebook, it is also true that I would not particularly admire a dinner invitation or a letter of condolence written so haphazardly. When we are unable to talk to someone face to face, our correspondence speaks for us. The impression it makes perhaps doesn't matter to dear friends, but it is very important to potential employers, places with which we do business, and casual acquaintances.

Accordingly, this book is designed to help you make the best on-paper impression possible. In this day of instant electronic mail, computerized desk-to-desk memos, and the convenience of the telephone, a well-written letter, personalized stationery, and traditionally and beautifully crafted invitations are truly a pleasure to the recipient. A sincere letter of condolence to a bereaved friend, a formal reply to a formal wedding invitation, a thank-you note instead of a commercial thank-you card—these are all ways of communicating that are especially meaningful.

Although our correspondence *could* be conducted on pages from spiral notebooks and on pre-printed cards, when it is, instead, handwritten on personalized stationery, when it expresses caring, thoughtfulness, a serious business statement, or the whimsical mood of the sender, then it makes a statement about who we are, and it is received as we intended it should be.

Should your last page of engraved, personal stationery be gone, however, don't wait two months for the order for more to be filled before letting someone know you care. By all means, use the back of an old grocery list and write. As Thomas Bailey Aldrich wrote to his friend Edward Sylvester Morse in the late 1800s, "There's a singular and a perpetual charm in a letter of yours; it never grows old, it never loses its novelty. . . ." Whatever the form, however illegible, a letter from a friend brightens everyone's day.

When writing to other than a close friend, of course the grocery list is unacceptable. By following accepted forms and using writing paper or invitations that reflect your good taste, you will find that you have a much better chance of getting the response and/or the results you desire. Your correspondence will reveal you as a man or a woman who takes the time to communicate the right way and who expects to be taken seriously.

Elizabeth L. Post
June 1990

Personal Correspondence

Q. *How do you choose personal stationery?*
A. Your choice is determined by a combination of your personal taste and suitability to the occasion. Everyone who does, or expects to do, any formal correspondence should have a supply of good-quality paper in a conservative color—usually white, ivory, gray, pale green, or pale blue—to be used for condolence notes, answers to invitations, and so on. This "good" paper need not be personalized, although it may have a monogram if you wish. It may be bordered in a conservative color, generally darker tones of the paper color or burgundy or gold or silver. It should not include design motifs, such as butterflies or kittens. Those papers should be reserved for informal notes and letters. The texture of the paper, whether it is rough or smooth, is a matter of personal choice, as is the texture of the edges, which may be moderately ragged to smooth. Most personal stationery produced by writing paper companies ranges from 5⅞ inches by 7¾

inches, called princess size, to 7¼ inches by 10½ inches, monarch size.

For more personal letters, there are no longer many restrictions, and color combinations may vary. A woman's paper may be marked with a monogram, initials, or her name and address. These may be placed in the center or upper left corner either in a contrasting shade or in a color to match a border. If stationery is monogrammed, either the single letter of her last name may be used or her three initials (with that of her first name to the left, her last name—larger—in the center, and her maiden name initial to the right). The paper is smaller than a man's, approximately 5½ inches by 6½ inches, and it may be a single sheet or a double, folded sheet.

Q. *Is men's stationery different from women's stationery?*

A. Men's stationery is larger, generally 7 inches by 10 inches to 7¼ inches by 10½ inches. Color and texture guidelines are those noted in the answer to the question above. It is folded in thirds to fit its envelope.

Q. *How is stationery personalized for . . .*
. . . married women?

A. A married woman's formal paper is engraved or printed "Mrs. Barry Farnham," rather than "Mrs.

Carolyn Farnham." For informal, personal letters she may have paper engraved "Carolyn Farnham," if she wishes. Women's stationery used for business correspondence may be marked with her professional name without title—"Sylvia Barrett"—rather than "Mrs. William Barrett."

Q. . . . *for single women?*
A. The name engraved or printed on an unmarried woman's paper is written without title—"Susan Foltin," never "Miss" or "Ms Susan Foltin." If engraved or printed envelopes are ordered, they may include "Miss" or "Ms" before the name in the return address.

Q. . . . *for divorced women?*
A. A divorcée's name may be preceded by whatever title she is using on the envelope (Mrs., Miss, or Ms), followed by her own first and last name, not the given name of her former husband.

Q. . . . *for men?*
A. When a man's stationery is personalized, it is usually marked in plain block or Roman letters at the top center. His name, without title (Mr., Dr., etc.), and his street address, city, state, and zip code all appear. His telephone number is optional. For purely social use, he may also have a family crest engraved or printed in the top center or the upper left-hand corner. If it is marked in the corner, his

name and address are engraved or printed in the right corner.

Q. *. . . for children?*
A. Children's stationery may be personalized with just a first name or with a first and last name. Mr., Master, or Miss should not precede the name.

Q. *Is it possible to get stationery for everyone in the household to use?*
A. Yes, and it is often very practical to do this instead of purchasing separate stationery for each person. Family stationery has the address engraved or printed in plain letters at the top. Frequently the telephone number is put in small type under the address or in the upper left-hand corner, with the address in the center. No names are included with the address.

Q. *I stayed with my uncle last summer and was invited to attend different parties with him. I was hesitant to use his stationery, which is printed with his address and phone number, in order to write thank-you notes to my hosts, but I didn't bring any of my own stationery along. When is it all right to use another's stationery?*
A. It would have been perfectly all right for you to have used your uncle's stationery for your thank-you notes, since it did not include his name, monogram, or crest. Naturally, it is considerate to ask first, but family or household engraved or printed

stationery is properly used by guests as well as by any family members.

Q. *Are there any guidelines you can offer to distinguish when to use stationery and when a fold-over note is sufficient?*
A. Fold-over notepaper is used for short notes to friends, for acceptances or regrets to informal invitations, and for informal invitations. Stationery is used for longer letters, for business correspondence, for letters of condolence, and for acceptances or regrets to formal invitations.

Q. *Should children have their own stationery?*
A. Yes. It helps make children consider letter writing a pleasure rather than a chore. Children's stationery is widely available at stationery stores. Usually it includes a design motif, which should be appropriate to the age of the child.

Q. *Where should the return address appear on the envelope—on the upper left-hand corner of the envelope or on the back flap?*
A. If the envelope is engraved, the return address is marked on the back flap because of the restrictions of the engraving process. However, the U.S. Postal Service prefers that the return address appear in the upper left-hand corner, so if the return address is printed or handwritten, it is preferable to follow Postal Service preference.

Q. *Must the return address be handwritten if envelopes don't have the return address printed on the back flap? Or may I use printed return address labels?*
A. You may use printed return address labels or handwrite your return address, whichever you prefer. You may also use labels even though the address is engraved on the back flap for business letters or other correspondence where it is important that the address be noticed.

Q. *Must formal stationery be engraved? Are other printing methods acceptable?*
A. Years ago, writing paper was engraved or it was not marked at all. Although a supply of paper with an engraved initial, monogram, or crest to be used for formal or special correspondence is very nice to have, today the cost of engraving has caused a change in thinking, and printed stationery is perfectly acceptable. Thermography is a printing process used as an alternative to engraving. The type is raised, and to the unpracticed eye it is indistinguishable from engraving. It is far less expensive than engraving, although more expensive than plain printing, where the letters are not raised.

Q. *May social letters be typewritten?*
A. There is no longer any rule against using a typewriter for most personal letters, but there are three types of letters that should always be handwritten unless you are disabled and cannot write with a pen. They are notes of condolence, formal replies to

invitations, and thank-you notes. If your thanks are a part of a longer, personal letter, the rule can be waived, and you could type the letter if you prefer.

Q. *Our family crest appears on my parents' stationery. I heard that, as the only daughter in the family, I shouldn't use the crest, but that my brothers can. Is this true?*

A. Yes, even today this is true. The crest is the exclusive property of male members of a family, although it may be used jointly by a husband and a wife on some occasions.

Q. *Addressing a letter to a couple used to be easy—the wife took her husband's name and that was that—but no more. Can you provide some guidelines for addressing letters to . . .*

. . . a husband and wife who don't use the same surname?

A. Address their letter to "Ms Monica Taggert and Mr. Hugh Huntington," or if they prefer, simply to "Monica Taggert and Hugh Huntington."

Q. *. . . a couple who live together but are not married?*

A. This couple's correspondence is addressed in the same way as for a married couple who don't use the same surname.

Q. *. . . a widow?*

A. A widow continues to use her husband's given name. She is "Mrs. Frederick Corry," not "Mrs.

Sarah Corry," which would indicate that she is a divorcee.

Q. . . . *a divorced woman?*
A. A divorced woman does not continue to use her husband's given name. She should be addressed as "Mrs. Elizabeth Seldon" unless she has followed an older custom, whereby a woman combined her maiden name with her ex-husband's last name. In that case, Elizabeth Northshield, who married and was divorced from John Sheldon, could become "Mrs. Northshield Seldon." If a divorced woman has taken back her maiden name, she uses the title "Miss" or "Ms," not "Mrs." When a woman is divorced more than once, she uses the name of her last husband with her own first name or with her maiden name—she does not use her former husband's name.

Q. *How are letters to government officials addressed?*
A. A business letter to the President of the United States is addressed "The President, the White House, Washington, DC 20500." The salutation is "Sir:" or "Madam:." A social letter is addressed either the same way or "The President and Mrs. Washington, the White House," etc. The salutation is "Dear Mr. President:," "Dear Madam President:," "Dear Mr. President and Mrs. Washington:," or "Dear Madam President and Mr. Black:."
A business letter to the Vice President of the

United States is addressed "The Vice President, United States Senate, Washington, DC 20510." The salutation is "Sir:" or "Madam:." A social letter is addressed the same way or "The Vice President and Mrs. Adams," home address, or "The Vice President and Mr. Adams," home address. The salutation is "Dear Mr. Vice President:," "Dear Madam Vice President:," "Dear Mr. Vice President and Mrs. Adams:," or "Dear Madam Vice President and Mr. Smith:."

A business letter to a United States senator is addressed "The Honorable Daniel Webster, United States Senate, Washington, DC 20510." The salutation is either "Sir:" or "Madam:." A social letter is addressed the same way or "The Honorable and Mrs. Daniel Webster," home address, or "The Honorable Jane Webster and Mr. Daniel Webster," home address. The salutation is "Dear Senator Webster:" or "Dear Senator and Mrs. Webster:" or "Dear Senator Webster and Mr. Webster."

A business letter to a member of the House of Representatives is addressed the same as one to a senator of the United States. A social letter is addressed the same as for a senator, except that the salutation is "Dear Mr. Clay:," "Dear Mrs. [Miss, Ms] Franklin:," "Dear Mr. and Mrs. Clay:," or "Dear Ms Franklin and Mr. Clay . . ." for a social letter.

Q. *I am often at a loss as to how to begin a letter. Have you any suggestions?*

A. All too often the social letters we write are months and months overdue, and we tend to begin with an apology for our tardiness. It is far nicer to say "You don't know, Eileen, how many letters I planned to write to you" than to say "I suppose you think I've been very neglectful, but I just haven't had a minute to get around to writing," which is actually unfriendly.

It is easier to begin a letter in answer to one that has recently been received. The natural beginning is "We were all so happy to get your letter" or "Your letter was so very welcome," followed by responses to various subjects in the letter you received.

A business letter should begin with a direct statement of the intent of the letter. If it is in answer to a letter, it may begin "In response to your letter of October 3, following is . . ."

Q. *Once I finally get around to writing to old friends, I find I go on and on or abruptly close with something foolish like "I'm sure I've bored you to tears by now." There is a better way to end a letter, isn't there?*

A. Of course there is. Just as the beginning of a letter should give the reader an impression of greeting, so should its ending express friendly or affectionate leave-taking. After responding to a friend's questions and comments, and sharing your own news, an ending such as "Will write again soon—you cannot imagine how much I miss you!" or "Counting the days till you get here" or "The ironing [or the bills, or the children, or a huge stack of reading for work] is calling and I can't ignore it any longer—will write again soon" are all friendly ways to end a letter that don't leave the reader with a feeling of abruptness or a sense that you couldn't wait to finish an unpleasant duty (writing to him or her).

Q. *Some people have a talent for writing letters that are a joy to receive. I wish I were one of them. Can you provide some guidelines for writing such letters?*

A. The letter we all love to receive is the one that carries so much of the writer's personality that he or she seems to be there with us. There are some things to keep in mind that make it easy to achieve a sense of *talking* through a letter. First, phrases typical of your speech should be used, not artificial formal language that is not natural to you. For example, if you would say "John is absolutely gorgeous and incredibly funny—I can't wait till you meet him!" write it. Don't say "John is an attractive young man with a good build who is often very amusing." Second, punctuation can add interest and variety to your letters in the same way as the change in the tone of a speaker's voice adds zest and color to a story. Underlining a word, using an exclamation point, inserting dashes as pauses in a long sentence—all give the reader a sense of hearing you speak. Next, remember that the use of contractions can make your writing natural. If you would not say "I do not know," don't write it. Write "I don't know." Occasionally inserting the name of the person to whom you are writing gives your letter an added touch of familiarity and affection. "And, Jeanine, guess what we are going to do this summer!" makes Jeanine feel that what you are writing is of special interest to her. Write as you think, as quickly as possible. This helps your letter seem as if you are truly talking to your friend.

Q. *When I write a long letter, I'm never sure if there are guidelines about numbering the pages. Can you enlighten me?*

A. One may write on both sides of single-sheet stationery if it is heavy enough that writing does not show through from one side to the other. Pages are numbered, beginning with page two, sequentially. Folded stationery sometimes causes confusion about proper page order. A two-page letter on folded stationery is usually written on the first (the front) and third pages. This leaves the second and the fourth, or outside back, page blank and prevents the writing from showing through the envelope. For longer letters, one may write pages one through four in regular order, or write on the first and fourth pages and then open the sheet and turn it sideways to write across the two inside pages as one. On fold-over or informal notepaper, when the address is at the top and there is nothing in the center, the note begins on the first page and follows into the center pages. The paper is opened flat and written on vertically as if it were a single page. If there is an initial, monogram, name, or design in the center of the front page, the note begins at the top of the opened center pages if it is long enough to cover more than half, and on the lower half if it is to be only a few words.

Q. *I always put the date on my letters; should I include my home address as well?*
A. If your stationery is not marked with your address, it is a good idea to provide it for your correspondent's convenience in replying. The upper right-hand corner of the first page of your letter is the usual place for your return address. You may also place it in the lower left-hand part of the page, just below the level of your signature. In either case, the date goes on the line directly below the address.

Q. *If I thank someone in person, must I also send a thank-you note?*
A. It depends on the circumstances. Thank-you letters are not necessary for presents that have been given in person on a birthday, at a house party, a shower, or other similar occasions when you have

directly spoken your thanks, although they are in no way wrong and may be written if you want to re-express your thanks. If the donor is not in attendance, a thank-you note is required. Thank-you notes are not necessary after a dinner party if you have thanked your hostess in person, or after a cocktail party or open house. Thank-you notes are also not required after an overnight visit with close friends or relatives whom you see frequently, but a telephone call to express additional thanks is obligatory.

Q. *Under what circumstances are thank-you notes obligatory?*

A. Thank-you notes are obligatory when you are the guest of honor at a dinner party, when you stay overnight at the home of anyone who is not a close friend or relative, and when the donor is not present when you open his or her gift. Thank-you notes are mandatory for all gifts you receive in the mail and for all wedding gifts. If you have been ill and have received gifts from friends, relatives, and associates, a thank-you note is required as soon as you are well enough to write it. When you receive notes of condolence, a thank-you is mandatory for all notes you receive but not for printed cards with no personal message included. Thank-yous must also be sent to those who have sent flowers, food, or fruit, or made donations to a charity in the name of the deceased.

Q. *What should I say in a thank-you note?*

A. Your note should be warm and appreciative and should either refer to the gift or the event specifically, not in general. Do not write "Thank you for your gift." Write "Thank you for the wonderful glasses! How we needed them—we were practically at the point of using paper cups." Do not write "Thank you for your hospitality." Write "Thank you for the lovely, lovely weekend. Tim and I feel so refreshed and relaxed after enjoying your warm hospitality." When someone has taken the time to try to select a meaningful gift for you, or has devoted time to entertaining you or hosting you, your thank-you should reflect a direct appreciation, mention something specific that was special about the gift or the event, and take a little of your time to create. A printed thank-you card with no personal message is never sufficient thanks.

Q. *When a gift comes from more than one person, to whom do you address your thanks?*

A. If the gift is from an entire family, address the envelope to "Mr. and Mrs. Jordan." The salutation is "Dear Nancy and Greg," with the children included in the text: "Please thank Brian and Diane for me, too, and tell them how much I like the picture frame." If the gift is from a couple, the thank-you may be addressed to both: "Dear Mr. and Mrs. Jordan" or "Dear Nancy and Greg." A dinner party thank-you is sent to the hostess, but thanks for an overnight visit are sent either to both husband and wife or to the wife, with the husband included in the text.

Q. *How do I thank someone for a gift of money?*
A. You should mention the amount, whether it is $5.00 or $500.00, and try to include the way you will use it—toward the purchase of a new chair, for example. If it is given with an intended use stated by the donor, be sure to respond accordingly: "What a treat to have $25.00 to spend on the baby—now we can get the carriage quilt we have wanted for so long!"

Q. *Have you any special suggestions for writing thank-yous for Christmas gifts?*
A. The most important suggestion is that the note be written within two or three days of the time the gift is received, but definitely before New Year's Day. As with other thank-you notes, a thank-you for a Christmas gift should name the gift and express enthusiasm and appreciation.

Q. *How soon after receiving a gift should the thank-you be written?*
A. Immediately. Someone who has sent a gift from a store or in the mail is anxious to know that it has arrived. If he or she does not hear from the intended recipient, it is easy to assume that it was never delivered, and the donor would want to try

to trace the gift. Thank-yous for wedding gifts also should be written as soon as the gift is received. If this is not possible, then they must be written as soon as the couple return from their honeymoon. For a very large wedding, when the gifts are innumerable, all thank-you notes should be mailed within three months.

Q. *When a gift is given to a baby or a very young child, should the thank-you note be written by the parent acknowledging the gift for the child or as if it were written by the child?*
A. Most definitely by the parent. A note "written" by the baby is too painfully cute and detracts from the sincere thanks that you really want to express for a special gift.

Q. *From the time they were little, I've always made my children write thank-you notes, and I saw to it they wrote them promptly. What can I do when others don't acknowledge gifts that were sent quite a while ago?*
A. This is no time to stand on ceremony. After three months, at the outside, you must write and ask whether or not the gift was received. It is *inexcusable* not to thank the donor for any gift, so if an inquiry from you is embarrassing to the recipient who received the gift but never bothered to acknowledge it, that is fine. Perhaps he or she will be more appreciative in the future.

Q. *In the very busy lives we lead today, is it acceptable to use printed thank-you notes?*

A. No matter how busy you are, someone else, doubtless equally busy, has taken the time to select a gift for you, perform a kind act, entertain you, or remember you in a special way. The least you can do is take three minutes and personalize a thank-you to him or her. If you do use a printed thank-you note, which is acceptable, you must add a few lines to it of specific thanks in your own words, not the words of the card company.

Q. *My husband and I recently received a simply horrible sculpture as a gift. Neither one of us likes it; how do we say thanks for something neither of us likes?*

A. With grace and charm. This is probably the most difficult thank-you letter to write, but there is no point in hurting the donor's feelings, although you need not lie. It is quite possible to find a phrase that can be taken to mean anything the recipient wishes. For example: "You can't imagine what a conversation piece the sculpture you sent us has become—everyone has a different interpretation of what it symbolizes, and it has generated some really lively discussion!" Or: "The little frog cream pitcher that pours from its mouth is simply fascinating. We've never seen one like it, and it delights the children" (which it probably does). The statements are not untrue, yet they indicate approval while not actually giving it.

Q. *I was in a bridal party recently where each of us received a lovely memento from the bride and groom. Since the memento was a thank-you for being in the bridal party, should we have written a thank-you to the bride and groom?*
A. Even though the gift is a thank-you to you, a note from you expressing your pleasure in the gift and in having been a part of the bridal party would be a nice, although not obligatory, gesture.

Q. *I recently received a promotion at work that was mentioned in the trade newspaper. Several former co-workers wrote to congratulate me. Do I write thank-you notes to each?*
A. Yes. All personal congratulatory cards and notes must be acknowledged, although congratulatory form letters from firms need not be answered.

Q. *What do you say in a letter congratulating a co-worker on a promotion?*
A. You state your pleasure in hearing the news of the promotion and express congratulations and warm wishes. For example:

> *Dear Ted,*
> *The news of your promotion was the best I've heard in a long time. We will miss you in the department, but everyone is genuinely happy for you. Congratulations on this most deserved promotion!*

Q. *We live in a small town. On the occasion of our recent wedding anniversary, it seemed as if the entire town sent us gifts, notes, and cards. There is no way we can possibly thank everyone personally, and it was suggested that we send a newspaper "card of thanks." Could you explain how this should be worded?*

A. In certain localities, most especially in small towns and rural areas, it is not only permissible but expected that recipients of a large number of gifts or kindnesses put a public "thanks" in the newspaper. Following is a typical "card of thanks:"

---

*We wish to express our thanks
to all those wonderful people
and organizations from whom we
received cards and gifts
on the occasion of our
fiftieth wedding anniversary
Sincerely,
Mr. and Mrs. Joseph Horne*

Even when a card of thanks is published, personal notes still should be written to those close to you who have gone out of their way to give something very special or to assist or participate in your celebration in any way.

"Cards of Thanks" are also used for occasions such as funerals, retirement parties, birthdays, political campaigns, and any other events that result in special kindnesses, assistance, gifts, or contributions.

Q. *I ordered something through the mail and I was not happy with the product I received. I want to return the product and obtain a refund. How do I write to complain?*

A. Keep in mind that the person who receives your letter will not be the one who made the error, and will be more disposed to make an adjustment if your letter is not irritating or insulting. State your complaint clearly and concisely, without being accusative or angry; note that the product is enclosed or being returned under separate cover; and say that you would appreciate an immediate refund. Keep a copy of this letter in case a follow-up is necessary.

If you would prefer a replacement item because your original order was damaged or broken when you received it, or if you wish to be issued credit rather than a refund, your letter should state your preference. You will generally get more satisfaction with a reasonable approach than with exaggerated accusations and anger. Merchandise does arrive broken, orders are confused, or goods are not of the quality advertised—all of which are legitimate reasons for complaint. Intelligent letters from customers pointing out these errors keep a company on its toes, and for the firm's own good should be given prompt attention. Following is an example of a sensible letter of complaint, containing all the necessary information.

March 30, 1990

Dear Sir or Madam:

On January 16 I ordered several Easter items from your spring catalog. When they had not arrived by two weeks before Easter, which was March 23, I called your customer service department and spoke with Miss Martin. She assured me that the items were to be shipped immediately. If they were, they did not arrive until today, March 30, and were useless to me since I had to substitute other items for those I had ordered. In view of the fact that ample time was given between my order and the expected delivery date, and since I can no longer use the items, I am returning them to you under separate cover and request that a credit be issued immediately to my Master Card, account number 23456890987, to which the original items were charged.

I thank you for your attention to this matter and ask that you send me a copy of the credit slip, for my records.

Sincerely,
Dawn Bollings

Q. *I've been asked to write a letter of recommendation, which I'm happy to do, but am not sure exactly what to say. Can you offer some guidelines?*

A. Letters of recommendation fulfill a specific function: to provide an honest evaluation of an individual whom you have come to know through your business or personal life. In general, a letter of reference should give the circumstances through which you know the person you are writing about and provide an evaluation of the qualities and abilities this person possesses. Relay any facts you think necessary to substantiate your evaluation. For example:

> It is a pleasure to recommend Jeanne Verrilli to you. During her five years here she was an asset to our auditing department and was instrumental in establishing our computerized inventory and warehousing operation. Her co-workers and supervisors continually praised her work and her ability to identify problems and to propose solutions.

The letter may end with an expression of your regret that she is relocating.

A letter of reference for a civic organization or membership in a club or professional association is addressed to the secretary and should mention your relationship with the person being recommended; his or her qualifications for membership (fund-raising experience, professional background, etc.); and an affirmation that this person will be a tremendous addition to the organization or club. For example:

> *I am delighted to propose Mr. W. Robert Connor for membership in the Lions Club. I have known him for nine years and consider him qualified in every way for membership. He serves on the Board of the University Club and has been actively involved in programs to provide opportunities for underprivileged youth. He is a graduate of Duke University and is a senior partner in the firm of Ivers and MacLellan. I know that Bob would be a great addition to our membership and hope that you will agree.*

Q. *In a moment of anger I said some hurtful things to a friend. The local card store has an "I'm sorry" card that sums up my feelings and the situation perfectly. Would it be okay to send such a preprinted card?*
A. Yes, often a preprinted card can express in illustration or in words thoughts that heal a rift, but you must add a few lines of your own to the card to personalize the message. Even a simple "I am really sorry—please forgive me, Love, Janet" lets your friend know the preprinted message is sincere and opens the door for you to call and make up after she receives the card.

Q. *What do you say in a condolence letter?*

A. A condolence letter is too personal for me to be able to give you a set form, with the exception of the only rule that should guide you in writing such letters. Say what you truly feel. Say that, and nothing else. Don't dwell on details or the manner of death or go on and on with a litany of sorrowful thoughts. The more nearly your note can express your sympathy, and a genuine love or appreciation for the one who has gone, the greater comfort it brings. If all you can think of is "Steve—what a wonderful man he was! I don't think anything will ever be the same again without him," say just that. Ask if there is anything you can do at any time to be of service. Just keep in mind that sincerity alone is of value, not flowery words or pages and pages of gloom.

Q. *My friend's grandmother was ill for a long time, and her death was not unexpected. How do you send condolences when death is a relief?*

A. This is difficult, because you want to express sympathy but cannot feel sad that one who has suffered so long has found release. Therefore, your expression of sympathy is not for the present death, but for the illness that started long ago. You might write: "Your sorrow during all these years—and now—is in my heart; and all my thoughts and sympathy are with you."

Q. *To whom should letters of condolence be written?*
A. If you knew the deceased well but do not know his or her family, the note is addressed to the closest relative—usually the widow, the widower, or the oldest child. It is permissible to add "and family" on the envelope when you are extending your sympathy to all rather than to just one person. When you did not know the person who died but do know one of his or her relatives, you write to that person rather than to someone who might have been more closely related. In writing to a married person whose parent has died, you may write only to the one whose parent it was, or to both.

Q. *My cousin's ex-husband recently died. Should I send a condolence letter to her or to her children?*
A. If they have maintained a friendly relationship, and you know that the survivor is truly upset by his or her ex-mate's death, naturally you should write. In most cases, however, the divorce indicates that they no longer wished to share each other's lives, so there is little need to send sympathy. The children of the divorced couple, even though they may live with the surviving parent, should receive notes if they have maintained a relationship with the deceased.

Q. *How should notes of condolence be acknowledged?*
A. In reply to hand-written, personal notes, you would reply in kind. Your note needn't be long. A

brief, "It meant so much to all of us to read of the special ways you remember Dad—thank you for writing," is all that is required. You may use the printed cards supplied by the funeral director only if you add a handwritten note to the printed words.

Q. *Is it correct to send change-of-address cards when we move, or is it necessary to write personal letters to everyone, giving them our new address?*
A. No, it is not necessary to write letters—you will hardly have time, in the middle of a move to write to everyone you know. You will save yourself countless hours of writing if you have change-of-address cards printed. There is no need to add a personal message to each one you send, although you certainly may. Change-of-address cards say simply:

After March first (or, On March first)
Mr. and Mrs. Howard Trumbull
will be living at (or, will change their address to)
Short Pine Farm
Craftsbury, Vermont 06572

If you send cards after you move:

Mr. and Mrs. Howard Trumbull
have changed their address to
Short Pine Farm
Craftsbury, Vermont 06572

If you know your new telephone number at the time you have the cards printed, it may be included, with the area code, under the address.

Q. *How do you feel about sending tape cassettes or videotapes in lieu of letters? Is it an acceptable form of "correspondence?"*

A. Of course it is. Although nothing can replace the written word as tangible evidence of love and remembrance, cassette and videotapes do something no letter can do—bring the sound of your voice or your image into the listener's or viewer's home that in turn brings a closeness that the written word cannot produce.

This is a special treat for older people who are often lonely and feel forgotten and neglected. To receive a tape (assuming the equipment exists to play it) makes the recipient feel as though he or she is with you. This means of communication also enables you to tell stories and news more fully than can be done in a letter. We used tapes to communicate with my father-in-law, who lived in Italy, and with our son and daughter-in-law when they were in the Peace Corps in Africa.

When receiving tapes in return, make some notes as you listen or watch, so you can remember what was said or done and comment on it in your reply.

Q. *Is it acceptable to send a commercial card of congratulation, or should a personal letter be sent instead?*
A. There is nothing wrong with sending a commercial card, but the card becomes a more personal expression of your feelings if you add a note. For example, if friends have announced the birth of a baby and you have purchased a "new baby" card, you might add:

> "Dear Margie,
>
>   We were so delighted to hear the news of Jonathan Junior's birth. Congratulations to all three of you!
>
>   I would love to come see you and the baby when I am next in town—I'll call and let you know when that will be.
>
>   Much love,
>   Lisa"

Q. *I have an aunt with whom I correspond, and her letters are always full of statements like, "The times seem to be getting worse and worse. I always said we would have to go through a long night before any chance of daylight. You can mark my words, the night is hardly more than begun." I don't know how to even begin to reply, so I have been ignoring her gloom and doom entirely. Should I acknowledge these statements in my letters?*

A. No useful purpose is ever served by writing needlessly of misfortune or unhappiness—even to members of one's family. It only serves to worry, irritate, or depress the recipients. It is polite to respond to comments made by one who writes to you, but you shouldn't reply in kind unless you feel as your aunt does. You could write, "I was sorry to read that you are so worried about the future, Aunt Rose. We all have to work hard to find the positive things around us, I guess. Something terrific happened to me yesterday. . . ." In this way, you acknowledge the feelings she expressed to you, but don't form your letter around her gloomy apprehension.

Q. *Are there any letters that shouldn't be written?*
A. There are two kinds of letters which especially should never be written. The first is a "love letter" or declaration of feelings to someone other than a spouse, which could be misinterpreted if the letter falls into the wrong hands. Letters that should never have been written are continually introduced as evidence in courtrooms, and many of them cannot, in any way, be excused. People foolishly write things that sound to a jury, for example, quite different from what was innocently intended. When the intent is not innocent—a letter alluding to details of an illicit romance, for example—harm could be

done not only to the writer and the intended recipient, but to other people in their lives, as well. Never write a letter to someone with the advisement to tear it up the minute they have finished reading it—he or she may not, leaving a permanent record, in your own handwriting, of something you would never want anyone else to know. Remember: Written words have permanence, and thoughts carelessly put on paper can exist for hundreds of years.

The second kind of letter that should never be written is an angry one. Anger in a letter carries with it the effect of solidified fury. Bitter spoken words fade away once the cause is forgiven; written words are fixed on the page forever. One point cannot be overstressed for both kinds of letters: Letters written under strong emotion should be held for twenty-four hours and reread before being sent—or, preferably, torn into small pieces and never sent at all.

Q. *Through the years, there have been many people who have extended themselves on behalf of me or someone in my family. These people range from service personnel to teachers at my children's school. I have always thanked them personally, but have wondered if I should let someone else know how appreciative I am. Could you give me samples of how I would do this?*

A. It is sad but true that people in general are quick to complain and slow to commend. Letters of complaint flow freely by the thousands; letters of praise trickle in by two's and three's. It is to your credit that you have thanked the people directly. It is to their credit when their supervisors know they have represented their business, school, or organization so well. It is also a thank you gift to the person who has extended him or herself for you to inform his or her supervisor.

When you are prompted to write a letter of commendation, first do your best to get the name of the person or persons who rendered the service, and the name or title of the person to whom you should write. Then describe the act or attitude that pleased you, and the date on which it occurred. A letter containing these specifics is of far more value, when commending a particular action, than a more general commendation. However, if you cannot remember or do not have all the details, a less specific letter will still be appreciated.

The following is an example of a letter of commendation for a specific action:

Brandt Tools, Inc.
4500 Main Street
Milwaukee, Wisconsin 53200

Mr. S.N. Jones
Manager, Flight Service
International Airways
Love Field
Dallas, Texas 75235

Dear Mr. Jones:
The normal conduct of my business takes me over a good part of the world via air travel, and from time to time there is an opportunity to write a complimentary letter about services that have been rendered.

Such a happy circumstance presented itself on January 26th on Flight 425 from Dallas to Phoenix, Arizona. The plane was full, and the three flight attendants in the coach section really did a job for you. They were not only efficient, but pleasant and cheerful to the point that it was really a pleasure to be on the flight.

The particular flight attendants involved were Sally Keene, based in Dallas; Juanita Velez of Dallas; and Gail Brooks, based in

Chicago. Will you please see that my thanks are
transmitted in some manner to these three
women.

> *Sincerely,*
> *Henry Dreyfus*
> *President*

A sample of a general letter of commendation
for a series of services or for a person's overall
performance would be the following:

> *31 Fulton Avenue*
> *Rye, New York 10580*
> *June 26, 1990*

Dr. Susan Klosek
Principal
Osborn School
Osborn Road
Rye, New York 10580

Dear Dr. Klosek:
 As you know, John and I were quite con-
cerned about Lydia's mid-year transition to Os-
born since our move was upsetting to her. Now,
just a few short months later, it seems as though
Lydia has always been an Osborn student. We
want to thank you for being so warm and wel-
coming, and want to thank all the faculty and

staff who helped make the adjustment for Lydia non-threatening and non-traumatic.

In particular, Mrs. Alfano has taken extra time with Lydia. Since there were curriculum differences and therefore some areas where she needed to catch up to the other students, Lydia could have experienced academic difficulty. Mrs. Alfano made sure Lydia had the resources she needed, and worked with her before school and during her lunch hour. As teachers ourselves, we know that those are break times a teacher really needs, and we will be forever grateful that Mrs. Alfano gave them up to help our daughter.

Please let her know how much we appreciate her dedication, kindness, and commitment, and please extend our thanks to Mrs. Codispoti, Mrs. Pullman, and Mrs. Hughes, as well. Each of them helped Lydia to feel comfortable in her new school.

Sincerely,
Mary Newling

Q. *Could you tell me how to write a letter requesting information?*

A. An information request should be brief and to the point. A reply is often expedited if you enclose a stamped, self-addressed envelope. Following is a sample information request letter:

> Meade Place
> Richmond, Virginia 23200
> April 12, 1990

Manager
Loon Lake Lodge
Shiretown, Maine 12267

Dear Sir or Madam:

　Would you be kind enough to send me your information folder and your schedule of rates for Loon Lake Lodge?

　I am also interested in what accommodations you have open for the month of August. We would require two double rooms with baths.

> *Sincerely,*
> *Madeline Newhouse*
> *(Mrs. Grant Newhouse)*

Q. *Is it possible to make a reservation by letter?*
A. Yes, it is, but it is a good idea to include your telephone number as well as your address, since many hotels require a credit card number or deposit before they will hold a reservation, and they may want to get in touch with you by telephone rather than by mail. You should not include your credit card number in the letter, however. A reservation letter might read:

> *6 Lakewood Avenue*
> *Jamestown, Virginia 23081*
> *October 3, 1990*

Framingham Hotel
Framingham, Massachusetts 01710

Dear Sir or Madam:
> *Will you please reserve a double room and bath for my husband and me for December 3rd through December 6th. We will arrive the evening of the 3rd, before 6 p.m. and depart the 6th before 11 a.m.*
> *If a room is not available for that weekend, please let me know at once so that we may make other plans. Otherwise, please confirm the reservation.*
> *Thank you very much.*
>> *Sincerely,*
>> *Barbara Anselmi*
>> *(Mrs. Robert Anselmi)*

Q. *When writing a letter which is confidential in nature, may I write "personal" on the envelope?*
A. In writing to someone at his or her home address you properly assume that no one else will open the letter. Therefore, it is rude to write "Personal" on the envelope. But if you are writing a social note to a friend's business address, it is entirely correct.

Q. *Recently I opened someone else's mail which was delivered in error to me. I never even looked at the name on the envelope. I re-sealed the envelope, but felt I should have explained. Is there any form to follow in this event?*
A. It is easy to open someone else's mail, particularly if you live in an apartment house where letters are often put in the wrong box, or if your name is a common one. When this happens, write, "Opened by Mistake" and your initials on the face of the envelope, seal it with a piece of tape, and put it in the mail.

Q. *We will have house guests for a week who will arrive before we return from a trip. I would like them to be able to use our club, which is permissible by club rules, but I don't know what form the request to the club should take.*

A. You would write a letter to the secretary or the manager of the club which reads to the effect of:

> *Dear Mr. Warren:*
>
> *I would appreciate it greatly if you would send a card extending the privileges of the club for the week of July 23rd for Mr. and Mrs. A.M. Stanton of Wilkes-Barre, Pennsylvania. The card may be sent to my address to the attention of the Stantons.*
>
> *Thank you very much.*
>
> *Yours very truly,*
> *Jasper Fletchworth*

Note the degree of formality. One does not write "Dear Jim," even if he is a close friend, because this is not a personal letter but a formal request to be put on file.

Q. *How should envelopes be addressed in correspondence to young people?*

A. Young girls are addressed as "Miss" socially from the day they are born until the day they marry or prefer to use the title "Ms." Both their first and last names are used on envelopes.

Boys may be addressed as "Master" until they are six or seven. After that, they are addressed without title until they graduate from high school or reach the age of approximately 18. At that time, they take the adult title of "Mr."

"Messrs." may not be used to address a father and son. It is correct only in writing to unmarried brothers, or to two or more business partners or members of a firm. Sisters may be addressed as "The Misses," but two unrelated women are addressed separately.

Q. *I receive a lot of seals from organizations to which I contribute money. I have never been sure exactly how they are used on envelopes, or when they are appropriate.*

A. Seals may be used on all personal and business letters. They should not be used on notes of condolence, or on formal invitations and replies. They are usually applied on the back of the envelope, covering the tip or end of the flap and the body of the envelope.

Business Correspondence

Q. *What is the correct form for a business letter?*
A. There are two acceptable forms for a business letter typed on company letterhead. The letterhead already includes the address of the company, so it does not need to be repeated. The first is with the date, the closing, the name, and the signature aligned to end near the right margin of the letter. The second is with those elements aligned at the left margin. Whichever is used, the spacing is as follows:

- The date appears at either the left or the right margin.
- The receiver's name appears six spaces below the date on one line, with his or her title on the next line and the company name, address, city and state on subsequent lines directly below the receiver's name.
- The salutation appears two spaces below the last line of the receiver's name and address.
- The text of the letter begins two spaces below the salutation.
- The closing appears two spaces below the

last line of the text of the letter, with the name of the sender aligned and typed four spaces below the closing.

- When a letter is typed by other than the sender, his or her initials appear after the initials of the sender, two lines below the typed name of the sender. The initials of the sender and the typist may be separated by either a colon or a slash.

- When there is an enclosure with the letter, it is indicated by typing the word "Enclosure" or "Enclosures (2)" on the line directly beneath the initials. The number in parentheses is optional and indicates the number of enclosures with the letter.

- If a copy of the letter is being sent to another person, it is indicated by typing "cc: John H. Hickey" on the line directly below the word "Enclosure." If there is no enclosure indicated, the "cc:" (which stands for carbon copy) is typed directly below the initials of the sender and the typist. If copies are being forwarded to more than one person, the names are aligned beneath one another:

  cc: John H. Hickey
       Charles W. Markham
       F. William Coleman

- If the sender's title is indicated on the letterhead, it would not be repeated beneath his or her typed name at the signature. If it is not included in the letterhead, then it would be included.

Following is a sample of a business letter with all elements aligned at the left margin:

April 5, 1990

Mr. Robert Armao

President

Armao & Company, Inc.

30 Rockefeller Plaza

New York, New York 10022

Dear Mr. Armao:

The Board of Directors of the Carnegie Foundation is meeting May 2, 1990 at 10:00 a.m. in the garden pavilion of the Foundation building. On behalf of the Board, I invite you to join us to present your proposal for Foundation distribution of funds as grants for several research projects.

Enclosed is the literature you requested on past Foundation projects.

We look forward to meeting with you on May 2nd.

Sincerely,

Franklin C. Scott

Chairman

FCS/bjt

Enclosure

cc: John F. Hickey

Charles W. Markham

The placement of the letter on the page, beginning with the date, and the width of the margins, depends on the length of the letter. A very short letter would be placed farther down on the page and have wider margins so that the letter would be more or less centered on the page.

A long, one-page letter would have narrower margins (never narrower than the width of the letterhead) and begin nearer the top of the page.

Adjustments may be made by decreasing the number of spaces from the letterhead to the date, and from the date to the name of the recipient. All other spacing remains the same.

Q. *What is a proper salutation for a business letter?*
A. When you know the person or know of the person to whom you are writing, the salutation is the same that you would use were you speaking to him or her—either "Dear Rich:" or "Dear Dr. Noonan:".

When you are writing to someone whose name you do not know, it has been traditional to address the letter "Dear Sir:" or "Gentlemen:". This greeting can be offensive to the recipient if she is a woman, however, so it is appropriate to address the letter "Dear Sir or Madam:". If you know the recipient is a woman but do not know her marital status, it is better to address your letter "Dear Ms. Walter:" rather than "Mrs." or "Miss." If possible, it is best to call the company and ask for the name and the proper spelling of the name of the person to whom you should address your letter.

It is also all right to address the person by the title of the job. For example, you could write "Dear Editor:" or "Dear Customer Services Manager:", although this can become unwieldy.

Recently, it has become acceptable to leave the salutation off the letter entirely, skipping two spaces and going directly to the text of your letter after the name of the company and the address.

Q. *If I want to indicate what a business letter is about, how should I do so?*

A. Between the name and address of the recipient and the salutation, type the letters "Re:" followed by the subject. This is typed two spaces below the address of the recipient and two spaces above the salutation "Re:" means regarding, and indicates at a glance for the recipient what to expect in the text of the letter:

> *April 5, 1990*
> *Mr. Robert F. Armao*
> *President*
> *Armao & Company, Inc.*
> *30 Rockefeller Plaza*
> *New York, New York 10022*
> *Re: Meeting of the Board of Directors*
>
> *Dear Mr. Armao:*
> *(etc.)*

Q. *How do I show my address if I am sending a business letter that is not on letterhead?*
A. To include your address when there is no letterhead, type it directly above the date, spacing it an appropriate number of lines down on the page to approximately center the letter on the page. It appears as follows:

> *6 West Avenue*
> *Larchmont, New York 10538*
> *July 2, 1990*
>
> *Mr. Branford Schaeffer*
> *The Portfolio Agency*
> *4141 Eastlake Avenue*
> *Chicago, Illinois 23415*
>
>
> *Dear Mr. Schaeffer:*
> (etc.)

If the right side of the page alignment is preferred, the placement would look like this:

> *6 West Avenue*
> *Larchmont, New York 10538*
> *July 2, 1990*
>
>
> *Mr. Branford Schaeffer*
> (etc.)

Q. *Are there any guidelines on the contents of a business letter?*

A. The content of business letters depends so thoroughly on the nature of the concern that it would be impossible to give examples to cover all possibilities. It should be said, however, that business letters should be clear, concise, and to the point. If you know exactly what you want to say and give considerable thought to the initial statement of your most important point, you cannot go far astray. When you have said what you intended to say, stop. A meandering last paragraph can destroy the entire effect of the letter.

If the recipient is a friend as well as a business associate, you may include one line of personal greeting at the end of the letter, but personal notes should not be interspersed throughout the letter.

Q. *What is the correct closing for a letter?*

A. The most often-used closing is "Sincerely."

Also correct are "Yours truly," "Very truly yours," and "Best regards." "Yours" is often used on informal office correspondence between close associates, but should not be used in general business correspondence between parties who are not familiar with one another. The term "Respectfully" is seldom used today. If it is used, it should only be on a letter from a tradesperson to a customer. It is also used at the close of minutes of a meeting or reports submitted for an organization's internal report and then it is generally used with the word "submitted," as in "Respectfully submitted," etc.

Q. *Should my signature include "Mr." or just my name? Should it be both my first and last name, or just my first name?*
A. You would use the same form as used in the salutation. If you opened with "Dear Jim," you sign your name "Frank." If you opened with "Dear Mr. Walters," you sign "Frank Boucher." You never include the titles "Mr., Mrs., Miss., or Ms." Your full name will always be typed four spaces below the closing.

If your name is exceedingly long, you may sign with initials to abbreviate the space the signature will take. For example, John Hunter Titherington Smith could sign "J.H.T. Smith" or "John H.T. Smith." Naturally, if he is writing a business associate with whom he is personally acquainted, he signs simply "John" over the typed "J.H.T. Smith."

Q. *I was recently married and have decided to use my husband's name professionally as well as socially. How do I sign business letters so recipients know who I am?*
A. For the first letters you send to associates who are not aware of your name change, use your first, maiden, and then married name in the typed signature of your letter. For example, Nancy Bullock who becomes Nancy Farnsworth would have typed "Nancy Bullock Farnsworth." After a period of

time, you may drop the maiden name and use a middle initial if you wish, or just your first and married name.

Q. *What elements should I look for when ordering business stationery?*

A. First, it should be attractive and of good quality, to indicate that the firm itself has and believes in those characteristics. The most versatile company stationery is a single sheet, white or off-white, measuring either eight by ten or eight and one-half by eleven inches. Both these sizes fit into the standard file, and folded into thirds, into regular business envelopes. The eight and one-half by eleven inch size is most convenient because it is the same size as standard paper used for copying machines. When it is to be used by various people in a company it includes the name of the firm at the top, with the address and telephone number, at either the top or the bottom of the page. If the company has a logo or emblem it regularly uses, this symbol is also included, usually at the top of the page with the name of the company.

If business stationery is to be personalized for executives in the company, their name and position are printed at either the left or right hand corner of the top of the page. If this is the case, the executive's position is not typed after his or her signature. Second sheets for business stationery are plain and are of the same paper as the first page.

Business envelopes for business stationery should always have the return address, with or without a logo and company name, printed at the left corner of the face of the envelope.

Q. *If business cards are enclosed with correspondence, what should they include?*

A. A standard form of business card for a salesperson or anyone not in an executive position has the name and address of the company printed in the center of the card with the employee's name in the lower left hand corner and the telephone number in the right hand corner, depending on the amount of space the company name takes and whether a logo is included. The name and telephone number may also be placed together in one lower corner, or in the upper corners. Both the weight of the paper used for the card and the color of the paper may vary, as may the color of the ink.

Hardway Container Corp.
16 Centre Street
Ames, Iowa, 50010

GEORGE DAVIS
SALES REPRESENTATIVE 515-555-3888

An executive has his or her name in the center, with his or her title centered under the name or in the lower left corner. The name and address of the company are put on the lower half of the card, either followed by the telephone number or with the telephone number to the right of the company name.

MARCIA HOLLIDAY
SALES MANAGER

High Tide Corporation
Columbus, Ohio 43200   614-555-7400

---

or

STEPHEN SUTPHEN

VICE-PRESIDENT
Rollins Engineering
Waynetown, Indiana 47899
317-555-1100

If the company has a separate FAX (facsimile) number, it should be listed underneath the telephone number.

Q. *Is there a standard size for a business card?*
A. Business cards are approximately three and one-half by two inches. Most business card files are set up to accommodate cards printed horizontally, although some businesses print their cards vertically.

Q. *When should a business card be included with correspondence?*
A. Usually, you would include a card the first time you send a business letter to someone with whom you will be in contact in the future. The enclosure of your card allows him to include it in his desk telephone file system so he has a ready reference to reach you either by telephone or by letter.

Q. *Is it acceptable to send holiday cards to business associates?*
A. Certainly. Many firms print a company holiday card in the name of the company. If this is the case, you would sign your name to the card. If your company does not follow this practice, you may have cards printed with your name or purchase cards and sign your name. The cards should be sent to the recipient at his or her business address, not to his or her home, unless the recipient is known to you socially as well as through business. If the card is sent to an associate's home, the name of the spouse is included on the envelope, whether you know the spouse or not.

All personal cards of this nature should be addressed by hand, nor should they be run through a postage meter but should have stamps affixed.

Q. *What form should I use to reply to a newspaper ad when I am looking for a job? I never know what salutation to use when all that is listed is a box number and an address.*

A. You use a business letter format, including your address and the date, followed by the address shown in the advertisement:

> *Box 324*
> *New York Times*
> *329 West 43rd Street*
> *New York, New York 10036*

The salutation is always difficult. Many people still begin a letter to an unknown recipient "Gentlemen:" which was standard practice for years. However, there is a 50% chance that the recipient is a woman. You may, therefore, begin "Dear Sir or Madam:" or you may avoid the problem altogether and eliminate the salutation. Type "Re: Your advertisement for sales manager" two spaces below the last line of the address. Skip two more spaces, and go directly to the text.

Q. *Is there a standard way to begin a letter which is in response to a newspaper ad?*

A. You should give a good deal of thought to the

phrasing of the opening sentence of your letter. It should engage the interest of the reader, who may receive hundreds of letters in addition to yours. Because a letter of application faces considerable competition, its chances of being read depend, to a great extent, on the way it establishes a favorable impression. In order for your letter to do this, you should pay particular attention to its physical appearance, and the manner in which it begins.

A standard response is, "Replying to your advertisement in today's *New York Times*, I am listing my qualifications below." This is not at all engaging.

Instead, state what you consider to be one of your important qualifications for the job. Write, "After five years of experience in operations and engineering, I feel that I am qualified to fill the position of director of operations advertised in Sunday's *New York Times.*"

Instead of writing, "I would like to be considered a candidate for the secretarial position which you advertised in Monday's *New York Times,*" write, "When I graduated from Katherine Gibbs in June, I was second in my class in stenographic and word processing proficiency. I believe you would find me an accurate, efficient, and dedicated worker."

Q. *Is it proper to send a follow-up letter when I have received no acknowledgement of my letter of application?*
A. Because newspaper advertisements often receive literally hundreds of responses, it is rare that the advertiser replies to each application submitted. You may certainly follow up. In fact, so few people do that your second message may attract more attention than the first. Your letter should be courteous and brief:

"On April 12, in response to your advertisement of April 10 in the *New York Times,* I submitted a letter of application for the position of director of operations. I am still quite hopeful that my application is being considered and that a candidate has not yet been chosen.

Would it be possible for you to let me know the status of my application?"

Q. *I recently received a reply to an application letter, indicating that the position for which I applied had been filled but that the company would keep my application on file. Should I send a thank you letter for their letter?*
A. If you are very interested in working for that company, then you may write again to express your appreciation for the consideration given your application:

"I want to express my appreciation for the careful consideration you gave to my letter of application dated April 12. Your reference to a possible increase in production next spring encourages me to believe that a vacancy in my field may occur at that time. If so, I wanted you to know of my continuing interest in working for DataElectronics.

I would like to take the liberty of writing you once again several months from now and enclosing an updated resume which would indicate my most recent experience.

Again, thank you."

Q. *I frequently have to handle correspondence to various professional people, and am never sure how to address their letters. Are there correct forms for such people as lawyers, doctors, dentists, or professors?*

A. A letter to an *attorney* would be addressed: "Robert Peck, Esq.", followed by the office address. The opening to the letter would be "Dear Mr. Peck," or "Dear Sir." If you were sending social correspondence to the home of the recipient, you simply write "Mr. Robert Peck," or "Mr. and Mrs. Robert Peck," excluding the "Esq."

A letter to a *physician* is addressed, "Bruce Sherling, M.D." and is headed "Dear Sir:" (or "Dear Madam:"). If you were addressing the correspondence to the physician's home, you would write, "Dr. and Mrs. Bruce Sherling" and begin the letter "Dear Dr. and Mrs. Sherling." If the woman is a doctor, correspondence sent to the home address would be addressed, "Mr. Reid Frost and Dr. Susan Frost," or just "Mr. and Mrs. Reid Frost" if she does not use her title socially. The salutation, if the title is used, would be "Dear Mr. and Dr. Frost." If both husband and wife are titled "Dr." you would begin, "Dr. Bruce Sherling and Dr. Ruth Sherling." The form for a *dentist* is the same as for a doctor, with the exception that the letters following the name for a business address are "D.D.S." instead of "M.D."

Correspondence to a *professor* is addressed either "Professor Stanley Sheldon," or "Mr. Stanley Sheldon." If the professor holds a doctorate degree and uses the title, then the letter would be addressed, "Dr. Stanley Sheldon." For a woman, it is either "Professor Miriam Hodge," "Mrs.," "Miss," or "Ms. Miriam Hodge," or "Dr. Miriam Hodge" if she holds a doctorate and uses the title. For social correspondence, the same titles are used. If the correspondence is being sent to the professor and his or her spouse at home, it would be addressed, "Mr. and Mrs. Stanley Sheldon," "Professor and Mrs. Stanley Sheldon," or "Dr. and Mrs. Stanley Sheldon," depending on the professor's preferred title; or "Mr. and Mrs. Paul Hodge," "Mr. Paul Hodge and Professor Miriam Hodge," or "Mr. Paul Hodge and Dr. Miriam Hodge." If both members of the couple are professors, you would address the correspondence according to their titles: "Professor Paul Hodge and Dr. Miriam Hodge," or "Professor Paul Hodge and Professor Miriam Hodge."

Q. *My new job entails writing to representatives of various religious organizations. Is there one particular address which may be used for all of them, or are there specific titles that should be used?*

A. There are specific titles, depending on which religious group it is, although correspondence to most *Protestant* ministers, priests, or pastors is addressed, "The Reverend William Kolb." The salutation is, properly, "Dear Sir," or "Dear Madam." For social correspondence, the salutations, "Dear Mr. Kolb," or "Dear Mrs. Jenkins" may be used for clergypersons without a degree. "Dr." would be used if a degree is held. If the title "Pastor" is used, it would be followed by the surname, as in "Dear Pastor Robbins."

A letter to a *Protestant Bishop* is addressed, "The Right Reverend Mark Haverstraw, Bishop of Illinois." The name may be followed by the Bishop's indication of degree, if known: "The Right Reverend Mark Haverstraw, D.D.," for example. The salutation is, "Right Reverend Sir:" for business, and "Dear Bishop Haverstraw" for social correspondence. A business letter to a *Rabbi* is addressed, "Rabbi Robert Rothman," or "Rabbi Robert Rothman, D.D." if he holds a degree and

it is known to you. As with Protestant clergypersons, the salutation is properly "Dear Sir:" or
"Dear Madam:". The salutation for a letter sent to
the Rabbi's home address is, "Dear Rabbi (or Dr.)
Rothman:".

A letter to the *Pope* is addressed: "His Holiness
Pope John Paul II" or, "His Holiness the Pope."
The opening to the letter is, "Your Holiness:".

A letter to a *Cardinal* of the Catholic Church
is addressed, "His Eminence John Cardinal O'Connor, Archibishop of New York." The business salutation is, "Your Eminence:" and the social salutation is, "Dear Cardinal O'Connor:".

To an *Archbishop* one would write, "The Most
Reverend Paul Cook, D.D., Archbishop of Los An-
geles," and begin the letter, "Your Excellency," or
"Most Reverend Sir:". A less formal or social letter
may begin, "Dear Archbishop Cook:".

A Catholic *Bishop's* letter would be addressed
in the same way, with the only difference being the
title used for social correspondence: "Dear Bishop
Franklin:".

To an *Abbot,* one would write, "The Right
Reverend Henry Smith," and begin, "Right Reverend Smith:" for business correspondence. For a less
formal or social letter, one would write, "Dear Father Abbot,".

Correspondence to a *Monsignor* is addressed,
"The Right Reverend Monsignor Burke:". The let-

ter opens, "Right Reverend Monsignor" for business correspondence, and "Dear Monsignor Burke" for less formal or social correspondence.

To a *Priest,* one addresses a letter "The Reverend Clark Murphy" followed by the initials of his order, if known. A business letter begins, "Reverend Father:" and a social letter opens, "Dear Father Murphy:".

Social Invitations

Q. *Throughout college we led a casual life and extended invitations by phone. Now business and civic activities demand greater formality, and we're not sure we are doing things correctly. How is an invitation worded for . . .*

. . . a formal dinner?

A. Private dinners that are formal enough to demand a third-person invitation are rare, but they do take place occasionally. An engraved invitation to a private dinner reads:

Mr. and Mrs. Mark Coleman

request the pleasure of your company

at dinner

on Saturday, the seventh of May

at half past seven o'clock

106 Waltham Street

Newton, Massachusetts 02165

R.s.v.p.

There are also fill-in, engraved cards that can be used for any occasion, including formal dinners:

Dr. and Mrs. Eugene Wasserman
request the pleasure of

Mr. and Mrs. Patrick Fulty's

company at *dinner*
on *Saturday, the second of August*
at *eight o'clock*
22 South Weymond
Athena, Oregon 97813

R.s.v.p.

If there is a guest of honor for the occasion, "To meet Mr. Stuart Ronk" is handwritten at the top of the invitation.

When the formal invitation to dinner or luncheon is handwritten instead of engraved, the wording and spacing must follow the engraved model's exactly.

Q. . . . *a private dance?*
A. The form most often used is:

Mr. and Mrs. Marc Balet
request the pleasure of

Miss Judith Espinar's

company at a dance
Friday, the first of November
at 9 o'clock
307 Summit Avenue
Leonia, New Jersey 07605

R.s.v.p.

If escorts or guests are to be included, the wording is: "request the company of Miss Polly Roberts and her escort's company at a . . ." or "Mr. Robert Turner and his guest." Titles are always used on formal invitations, including "Miss," which is not used on wedding invitations but is used on other invitations.

If the invitation is to a dance in honor of a person or an event, this information is included on the invitation:

Mr. and Mrs. Douglas Jones
request the pleasure of your company
at a dance in honour of their niece
Miss Rosemary Allen
Monday, the seventeenth of January
at ten o'clock
The Hyatt Regency
Cambridge, Massachusetts
Please reply to
219 Hornbine Road
Rehoboth, Massachusetts 02769

Note that if the address to which replies are to be sent appears on the envelope or if it follows "R.s.v.p." on the invitation, the ZIP code is not included in the body of the invitation.

Q. . . . *a charity benefit?*

The Directors of the University Club
invite you to subscribe to
The Spring Ball
to be held at
The University Club
on Saturday, the fifth of April
Nineteen hundred and ninety
at ten o'clock
Evanston, Illinois
R.s.v.p.

When the expenses are to be covered by the sale of tickets, these invitations are accompanied by a card stating the amount of the subscription, where it should be sent, and so on. Names of the committee members, debutantes being presented, or sometimes the patrons are printed inside the invitation.

Q. . . . *a public ball?*
A. Usually, this kind of event is given by a committee for a charity or by a club or association to benefit another organization. The invitations are accompanied by response cards, lists of patrons, and cards with pertinent information. One does not need to refuse this type of invitation. The return of the filled-in response card and the check for the tickets constitute an acceptance. The invitations are worded:

The Executive Directors of the Ocean Club
request the pleasure of your company
at a Ball
to be held at the clubhouse
on the evening of Thursday, the first of July
at nine o'clock
for the benefit of
United Hospital Medical Center

Single Ticket $45.00   *Black Tie*
Couple $75.00

Q. . . . *a reception or a tea?*
A. For these events, a time is not set at a certain

hour, but is limited to a definite period indicated by a beginning and a terminating hour. An invitation to a tea for a debutante would read:

Mrs. Marvin Henk

Miss Erin Henk

will be at home

Tuesday, the sixth of February

from five until seven o'clock

850 Fifth Avenue

Except for very unusual occasions, a man's name does not appear. Mr. Henk's name would appear with that of his wife if he were an artist and the reception were given in his studio to view his work, or if a reception were given to meet a distinguished guest, such as a governor or a bishop. In this case, "In honor of the Right Reverend William Lazerus" or "To meet His Excellency, the Governor of Nebraska" would be engraved at the top of the invitation. Suitable wording for an evening reception would be:

To meet the Honorable Anthony Demarest

Mr. and Mrs. Marvin Henk

at Home

Thursday, the fifteenth of September

from nine until eleven o'clock

850 Fifth Avenue

Q. *. . . an affair with more than one host?*

A. Confusion may occur if the invitation does not make very clear where the event is to take place, and where the acceptances and regrets are to be sent. For example, if a dinner is to take place at a club or restaurant, the form is this:

Mr. and Mrs. Darcy Gibson

Mr. and Mrs. Edward Johnson

Mr. and Mrs. Ralph Rogers

request the pleasure of your company

at dinner

Friday, the fourth of March

at half after seven o'clock

at

Manursing Island Club

R.s.v.p.

Mr. and Mrs. Darcy Gibson

Pinegrove Farm

Waverly, Pennsylvania 18471

If, on the other hand, the event should be a luncheon at Mrs. Gibson's house, the correct form would be this:

Mrs. Darcy Jamison Gibson
Mrs. Edward Adam Johnson
Mrs. Ralph Edward Rogers
request the pleasure of your company
at a luncheon
at half after one o'clock
Pinegrove Farm
Waverly, Pennsylvania 18471
R.s.v.p.
Mrs. Darcy Jamison Gibson

There is no rule about the order in which the names of two or more hostesses should appear, except that the one at whose house the party will be held is usually placed first. Or if one is a great deal older, her name may head the list.

If there is no R.s.v.p. name or address, send your reply to the first hostess listed.

Q. . . . *an informal party?*
A. Invitations to an informal occasion may be sent in the form of a note written on an informal or on fill-in invitations, available at stationers. The telephone is also a perfectly acceptable means of extending an informal invitation.

you are invited by

for

on   at   o'clock

at

Q. *What sort of written invitations should I select for a formal dinner party? Can they be typewritten?*
A. Handwritten invitations to a formal party should be on plain white or cream notepaper or paper stamped with a very small monogram or with the family's crest. The wording and spacing must follow the engraved model's exactly. They may not be typewritten. You may also use fill-in invitations if the printed part adheres to the standards for fully printed or engraved invitations.

Q. *What does a third-person formal invitation look like?*
A. They look like an invitation for a wedding reception and are either engraved, printed, or handwritten on plain or plate-marked cards, white or cream. Cards generally vary in size from 6 inches by 4½ inches to 3 inches by 4 inches. Postal regula-

tions are that mailing envelopes be at least 3½ inches high by 5 inches wide.

The lettering is a matter of personal choice. The plainer it is, the easier it is to read. Punctuation is used only when words requiring separation occur on the same line, and in certain abbreviations, such as "R.s.v.p." The time is given as "half past seven o'clock" or "half after seven o'clock," never as "seven-thirty."

Since the vast majority of parties given today are not formal, the hostess who wishes her guests to dress formally must indicate this on her invitations. The phrase "black tie" should appear in the lower right-hand corner of invitations to proms, charity balls, formal dinners or dances, evening weddings, or any event to which a wide assortment of people is invited.

Q. *Are titles used on formal invitations?*
A. Always, for man, woman, or child.

Q. *How do handwritten formal invitations differ from engraved invitations?*
A. They do not differ. The wording and spacing on a handwritten formal invitation must follow exactly as they would for an engraved invitation.

Q. *What is an informal? Is it acceptable to use informals as invitations?*
A. Informals are small, fold-over cards. Plain infor-

mals are available at all stationers. If you wish, however, you may have them engraved, thermographed, or printed with your name or with your
monogram in the upper left corner. Or "[Mr. and]
Mrs. James Cutler" across the center. Envelopes
for informals must be 3½ inches by 5 inches. Informals may be used as invitations. If the card is engraved with your name, the invitation is written in
this way:

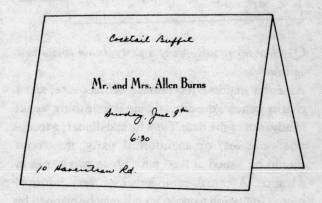

Cocktail Buffet

Mr. and Mrs. Allen Burns

Sunday, June 9th
6:30

10 Havenstraw Rd.

If the informal is only monogrammed or entirely unmarked, the invitation takes the form of a
brief note and must include your name, since the
recipient may not know by whom it was sent. You
may, if you prefer, put "Regrets only," followed by
your telephone number or address, instead of
"R.s.v.p." on all informal invitations.

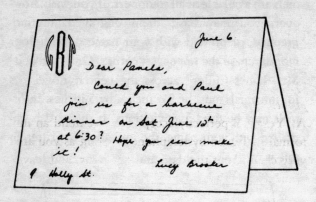

Dear Pamela,

Could you and Paul join us for a barbecue dinner on Sat. June 13th at 6:30? Hope you can make it!

Lucy Brooker

9 Holly St.

Q. *How far in advance of a party should invitations be issued?*

A. For a wedding reception, a ball, a dance, and a charity benefit, the usual timing is four to six weeks in advance of the date. For a formal dinner, a reception or a tea, or an informal party, invitations should be issued at least ten days to two weeks in advance. A casual get-together or very informal dinner invitation to close friends may be planned by telephone anywhere from a week ahead to the very same day for a spur-of-the-moment invitation.

Q. *We received an invitation on a commercial, fill-in card, worded in the third person. Do we reply as if it were a formal invitation?*

A. No. Even though these invitations are worded in the third person, they are not formal invitations and need not be answered as such. A brief note or your own informal with a note of acceptance or regret, or a telephone call, if the number appears in the invitation, are all acceptable forms of reply.

Q. *Is it ever acceptable to issue an invitation by telephone?*
A. Yes. It is perfectly acceptable to extend an informal invitation by telephone, so long as you are very clear about the date and the hour, and leave your guests in no doubt about what is intended.

Q. *If a cocktail party is held before a dinner dance or other function, may a guest accept the invitation to the first event but not the second?*
A. No, the invitation to a cocktail party should not be accepted if you do not intend to go on to the later event unless the hostess specifically says, "Please join us first, even though you can't come to the club afterward." It is not up to you to make this suggestion except when the hostess is a very close friend, in which case you may say, "We'd love to stop by for one drink, but we are going to dinner at the Burkhardts'."

Q. *Do the invitations to a cocktail buffet differ from invitations to either a cocktail party or buffet?*
A. Yes, in that it should be made very clear that the gathering is a "cocktail buffet," so that guests realize that they will be served some substantial food

and need not make other plans for dinner. The invitation frequently states only the hour of arrival, with no ending time, because guests are expected to linger longer than if a party is just a cocktail party.

Q. *What do BYOB and BYOF mean on an invitation?*

A. "BYOB" means "Bring Your Own Bottle." The host provides food and mixes for drinks, but the guests are asked to bring whatever they want to drink. The bottles brought to these parties are not intended to be gifts for the host and hostess. They simply make it possible for the group to get together without anyone having to incur an enormous expense. Therefore, you may initial or mark your bottle and take home any liquor that is left.

"BYOF" means "Bring Your Own Food." Invitations to these parties do not simply state "BYOF." The hostess who arranges this sort of evening is not giving the party, she is organizing it. On a written invitation, she would ask each guest to bring a specific dish, or she would note "Pot-Luck Dinner" or "Chip-in Dinner" at the top. If the invitations are made by telephone, the hostess must be very clear about what is expected. Unless the invitation specifies a dish and a bottle, the hostess is expected to provide liquid refreshment.

In both cases, the intent should be stated immediately so that no misunderstanding occurs. A guest may resent accepting an invitation to a party only to find out after accepting that he or she is expected to contribute, whether the contribution be liquor, food, or money. Someone who is unwilling or unable to contribute may feel trapped when told the arrangements after accepting.

Q. *What are reminder cards? When are they used?*
A. They are written reminders of an event to which a guest has been invited by telephone, verbally, or several weeks before by mail. You simply write on an informal or on notepaper: "To remind you—Wednesday 10th, 7:30" or "Dear Jane, just to remind you that we are expecting you and Tom on the fifth. Can't wait to see you."

Q. *What are answer cards?*
A. Answer cards are enclosed with invitations to ensure invited guests will reply to the invitation. They are usually small and engraved in the same style as the invitation, with a box to check that indicates whether the invited guest will attend or not. Invitations to private parties often include a self-addressed, stamped envelope with the card. When answer cards are included with the invitation, a formal reply need not be sent as well. It is not wise to have a space for the invited guest to fill in that reads "Number that will attend," since some recipients may take that to mean that children, house guests, or anyone else may be included in the invitation.

Mr. Warren Harris

☐ accepts

☐ regrets

Friday, January second
Columbus Country Club

M _____

will _____ attend

Friday, January second

Q. *When an invitation has to be recalled, what form is used? Is the reason for the recall of the invitation given?*

A. The form, if time permits, is a printed card that states the reason. For example:

> *Owing to the illness of their daughter*
> *Mr. and Mrs. Theodore Fremd*
> *are obliged to recall their invitations*
> *for Friday, the sixteenth of May*

When an engagement is broken after the wedding invitations have been issued:

> *Mr. and Mrs. Ferdinand Mapes*
> *announce that the marriage of their daughter*
> *Barbara Jill*
> *to*
> *Mr. David Hill*
> *will not take place*

In an emergency, the message may be handwritten or given by telephone.

Q. *Is it permissible to ask a hostess to extend an invitation to someone?*

A. No, unless the invitation is for a buffet or reception where one or two unexpected guests would probably make no difference. If this is the case, you must telephone so that you can explain your situation and the hostess can either say "Of course, do bring your guest" or "I'm sorry, but we simply have no more room!" When regretting an invitation because you have guests, you may always explain that you are expecting guests. If the hostess says, "Do bring them—I would love to meet them," you may, but you may not suggest it yourself.

Q. *Is it okay for one member of a couple to accept an invitation and the other to decline? How would the response be worded?*

A. Yes, it is perfectly acceptable to take for granted that either one of an invited couple would be welcome if the other wasn't able to attend. In response to a formal invitation, the response would be worded:

> *Mrs. Stephen Haynes*
> *accepts with pleasure*
> *Mr. and Mrs. Jamison's*
> *kind invitation for*
> *Saturday, the sixth of March*
> *at eight o'clock*
> *but regrets that*
> *Mr. Haynes*
> *will be unable to attend*

If it were Mrs. Haynes who could not attend, the wording would merely transpose the "Mr." and "Mrs."

In response to an informal invitation, a note of explanation should be sent, such as "I would love to be at your dinner party on the sixth but will be coming without Stephen, who will be out of town."

Q. *If an invitation contains a reply card, can a personal note be sent instead?*
A. No, when a response card is sent with the invitation, it should be used for the reply, not a handwritten response. Very often the hostess keeps a filing box for response cards and does not wish to receive answers in a variety of shapes and sizes.

Q. *How soon after receiving an invitation should I reply?*
A. Instantly, or as soon as is possible. It is inexcusably rude to leave someone who has invited you with no idea of how many people to expect. If the R.s.v.p. is followed by a telephone number, do your best to call promptly. If you cannot get through after several attempts, send a brief note or even a postcard with your acceptance or regrets.

Q. *How is a formal reply worded?*
A. Your reply matches the invitation, which makes it very easy to write:

> *Mr. and Mrs. Zachary Scott*
> *accept with pleasure*
> *the kind invitation of*
> *Mr. and Mrs. Patrick Coppolla*
> *for dinner*
> *on Monday, the fifteenth of December*
> *at eight o'clock*

Your reply may also say:

> . . . *accept with pleasure*
> *your kind invitation for* . . .

The formulas for regret are:

> *Mr. and Mrs. Zachary Scott*
> *regret that they are unable to accept*
> *the kind invitation of*
> *Mr. and Mrs. Patrick Coppolla*
> *for Monday, the fifteenth of December*

or

> *Mr. and Mrs. Zachary Scott*
> *regret that they are unable to accept*
> *Mr. and Mrs. Coppolla's*
> *kind invitation for dinner*
> *on Monday, the fifteenth of December*

In accepting an invitation you must repeat the day and the hour so that any mistake can be rectified, but if you decline, it is not necessary to repeat the hour.

Q. *To whom is the reply to a formal third-person invitation addressed?*
A. The reply is addressed to the person or persons from whom the invitation comes. The full first

name, rather than initials, is used, and the name of the state is also written out in full. A return address should appear on the back flap of the envelope.

Q. *How does one know where to send a reply?*
A. One sends a reply either to the address shown on the invitation or to the address which follows the R.s.v.p. if the event is to be held at one place and the replies received at another. If the address appears in neither place, then replies should be sent to the return address shown on the envelope. If you do not find an address on an engraved invitation, be sure to check the back flap of the envelope, where the address may be embossed (raised) but not printed.

Q. *I received an invitation with an R.s.v.p. followed by a telephone number. May I still respond through the mail?*
A. Yes, of course, as long as you respond promptly and for some reason are unable to call or cannot get through by telephone.

Q. *What is the difference between "R.s.v.p." and "Regrets only"?*
A. "R.s.v.p." means a response is requested, whether you are able to attend or not. "Regrets only" means that you are to respond only if you will not be able to attend. It is assumed if the host or hostess does not hear from you that you will attend.

Q. *May informals be used for replies?*

A. Certainly, if the invitation is issued in an informal, fill-in, or semiformal fill-in manner, even if the semiformal fill-in invitation is worded in the third person. You may use your informal, as illustrated below, or you may write a sentence on your notepaper or a postcard. All you need say is "Thanks so much—we will be there on the 10th."

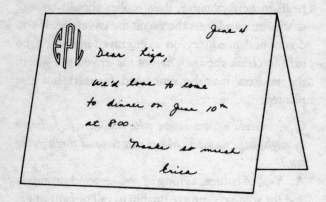

Q. *We received an invitation to a public charity ball but are unable to attend. Must we respond and, if so, how?*
A. No, one does not need to refuse this type of invitation. In this case, the only replies expected are from those who will attend. If you were to attend, the return of the filled-in response card and a check for tickets would constitute your acceptance.

Q. *When more than one person hosts a dinner, how is the reply worded and to whom is it sent?*
A. Your response includes all the names that appear on the invitation, even though the envelope is addressed only to the name following the R.s.v.p., or the first name on the list of hostesses.

> *Miss Helen Moore*
> *accepts with pleasure*
> *the kind invitation of*
> *Mrs. Chalmers and*
> *Mrs. DeSoto and*
> *Mrs. Pinney*
> *for Wednesday, the third of June*
> *at half after one o'clock*

The invitation should make very clear, following the R.s.v.p., where acceptances and regrets are to be sent. If for some reason it does not, then the reply should be sent to the person at whose house the party is to take place, whose name is usually first on the list. If the party is to be held at a hotel or a club and there is absolutely no indication of where an R.s.v.p. is to be addressed, you must send your reply to all the hosts at the hotel or club.

Q. *I don't drink alcoholic beverages. Should I tell my hosts I don't drink when I accept? Or should I decline cocktail party invitations?*

A. There is really no need to either announce that you don't drink alcoholic beverages or to miss parties because you don't, unless you are a teetotaler for moral reasons and disapprove of drinking in general. If you simply choose not to drink and it is not a moral issue, then by all means accept the invitations you receive. Every good hostess has soft drinks of some kind available, and certainly has water. If you are worried that there will be nothing for you to drink, take a bottle of your favorite soda along. Leave it in the car unless you find that there is literally nothing you can drink in the house.

Q. *What are valid reasons to change an acceptance to a regret?*

A. There are three valid reasons: illness (yours, a child's, or someone in your household's); death in the family; or a sudden, unavoidable trip.

Q. *How do I change my response to an invitation: From no to yes? From yes to no?*

A. When you have refused an invitation and then

find that circumstances have changed, enabling you to attend after all, you may call the hostess, explain your situation, and ask if you may change your regret to an acceptance—but only when the invitation is to a wedding, a large reception, a cocktail buffet, a picnic, or any affair at which another guest or two would not cause any complications. If the invitation is to a theater party, a seated dinner, or an evening of bridge, you should not call, since the hostess would surely have filled your place, and it would embarrass her were you to ask to be reinstated and she had invited someone else.

When you have accepted an invitation and find, because of pressing circumstances, that you cannot attend, it is essential that you let the hostess know immediately. In most cases, a telephone call is best—it is quick, and gives you a chance to explain your problem and express your regrets. If there is ample time, you may write a short note, giving the reason and your apologies.

Q. *An unexpected business trip forced one of my guests to cancel her acceptance two days before my dinner party. Would it have been proper to ask a friend to fill in?*

A. Yes, it is perfectly proper to call a friend and explain, inviting him or her in the stead of the guest who canceled. This friend should be flattered that you are asking, not upset that he or she was not included in the first place.

Q. *Should I mention my diet to my hostess when accepting her invitation?*

A. No, in most cases you would not mention your diet at the time you accept the invitation, since this would make your hostess feel obliged to change the menu or prepare something special for you. If you are a vegetarian, for example, you may either put a very small amount of meat on your plate and leave it there or you may tell the hostess, when you arrive, the reason you will not be eating the meat so that she is not concerned. You should never feel it necessary to eat anything that is injurious to your health or contrary to your moral standards. If you have a strict diet based on moral reasons, it is better to discuss it with your hostess beforehand. If it is a formal, "public" dinner, you might have to refuse the invitation, but if it is a small gathering of friends, you can tell the hostess you will bring a dish for yourself, prepared according to your restrictions.

Q. *What does it mean when an invitation specifies a certain type of dress? Just what do "white tie," "black tie," "formal," and "semiformal" mean?*

A. When an invitation specifies a certain type of dress, it means that it is expected that guests will dress according to the specification. "White tie" specifies the most formal evening wear—white tie, wing collar, and tailcoat for men; formal evening

gowns for women. "Black tie" or "formal" specifies ordinary formal evening wear—a tuxedo with
a soft shirt and bow tie. A dark suit is not an acceptable alternative. If a man does not own one, he
should rent a tuxedo for formal occasions. Tuxedo
jackets may be patterned, other colors beside the
traditional black, or white in the summer only.
"Black tie" for women means dressy dresses, cocktail length or long evening wear, depending on
local custom. "Semiformal" on invitations means
sport jackets or suits for men, and dresses or dress-
ier tops and pants for women, never jeans or
T-shirts for either.

Q. *How should the announcement of the adoption of
our baby be worded? May we use a commercial birth
announcement?*
A. You may either write or have printed an announcement, or you may use a commercially produced announcement. If you select the latter,
choose one in which you can easily insert the words
"adopted" or "adoption" in the wording. Also
make sure the announcement is appropriate to the
child's age. For example, don't select a card with a
picture of a stork with a baby in it's mouth to announce the arrival of your two-year-old adopted
son.

 If you choose to have printed or write your
own announcement, the wording could be:

Mr. and Mrs. David Newkirk
have the happiness to announce
the adoption of
Sarah
age, thriteen months

If you have adopted a newborn, you may include all the vital statistics usually included on birth announcements, including date, weight, length, etc. One of the nicest announcement cards designed for sharing the news of two adopted children was this one, sent by a family who already had a son and a daughter.

Every Child Comes with a Message
That God is Not Yet
Discouraged of Man
—TAGORE

Michael, Angela, Peter and Eileen Allen
are proud and happy to announce
the adoption of

a daughter and a sister	a son and a brother
Judith Ellisor	*Jonathan Spencer*
born June 28, 1982	born July 16, 1983

arrived from Laos—December 12, 1984

Q. *What kind of invitation should I use for my baby's christening?*

A. Usually, christening invitations are given over the telephone or by personal note. All invitations to a christening should be very friendly and informal:

> *Dear Linda,*
> *Michael will be christened on Sunday, the 24th, at 3:00 in Christ Church. Would you and Ted come to the ceremony at the church, and join us afterward at our house?*
>
> *Love, Martha*

A message may be written on an informal note, instead, simply saying, "Michael's christening, Christ Church, March 24, 3 o'clock. Reception at our house afterward."

Q. *How should friends and family be invited to a brit?*

A. Invitations are usually made by telephone, since the time between the baby's birth and the ceremony is short.

Q. *May formal invitations be sent for a Bar or Bat Mitzvah?*

A. Yes. Invitations may be third-person formal if the party celebrating the Bar or Bat Mitzvah is formal, or handwritten notes if it is not. Invitations to an informal reception may also be telephoned. As with other invitations, they must be acknowledged promptly, and in kind.

Mr. and Mrs. David James Rosenfeld
joyfully invite you
to worship with them
at the Bar Mitzvah of their son
Howard Steven
Saturday, the twenty-first of July
Nineteen hundred and ninety
at ten o'clock in the morning
Congregation Ben David
3802 Hollywood Boulevard
West Hollywood, California

Q. *Because space is limited, only two guests may attend my daughter's graduation ceremony. May we send announcements of her graduation? We don't want people to feel obligated to send gifts.*

A. Yes, you may send announcements. The restriction on the number of invitations most schools impose has led to an increase in graduation announcements. You should send them only to close family and friends, however, who would want to send a gift. Although graduation announcements *should* carry no obligation for the recipient to send a gift and are intended only to share good news, most people do feel obligated to give one. Therefore, if you want to send announcements to a wider range of friends, you may write "No gifts, please" at the bottom of the announcement.

Q. *How should invitations to an anniversary party be written?*

A. The form of the invitations depends entirely on the degree of formality of the party. They may range from an informal telephone call to an engraved, third-person invitation. In between lie the most common forms—handwritten notes or informal, fill-in cards. Formal invitations for a twenty-fifth anniversary are often bordered and printed in silver; those for a fiftieth, in gold. When a couple gives an anniversary party themselves, one form of invitation could read:

1965–1990

Mr. and Mrs. Edward Peyton

request the pleasure of your company

at a reception

in honor of

their silver wedding anniversary

on Saturday, the eighth of December

at eight o'clock

Wildwood Country Club

R.s.v.p.

12 Windmere Road

When the children of the couple give the party, their names or relationship should be indicated.

1940   *1990*

The Children of
Sally and George S. Denver
request the honor of your presence
at the
Fiftieth Anniversary
of the marriage of their parents
on Saturday, the twenty-fourth of November
nineteen hundred and ninety
at eight o'clock
Gramercy Park Hotel
New York, New York

A printed invitation could read:

In honor of the
fiftieth wedding anniversary of
Mr. and Mrs. Arthur Newberry
Mr. and Mrs. John Newberry
and
Mr. and Mrs. Bradley Bruce
[or Their Sons and Daughters]
request the pleasure of your company
on Saturday, the seventh of July
at seven thirty o'clock
Appawamis Club
Holyoke, Massachusetts

R.s.v.p.
45 Mount St. James
Syracuse, New York 13210

An informal note from the children of the couple might read:

"Dear Mrs. Vose,
Will you and Mr. Vose join us for dinner at the Hunt Club on Saturday, September 5, at 7:00 p.m., to help us celebrate Mom and Dad's twenty-fifth anniversary? Hoping to see you then."

Q. *My brothers and I are planning a fiftieth wedding anniversary party for our parents. We know that they would not want their friends to bring gifts, but will just be happy to see everyone. How do we indicate this?*

A. Simply write, "No gifts, please" at the end of the invitation.

Wedding Invitations

Q. *When should invitations be ordered?*
A. Invitations to a large wedding are sent four to six weeks beforehand, and most printers require four to six weeks for engraving, thermography, or printing. Therefore, it is best to order invitations at least twelve weeks before the wedding.

Q. *What is the traditional style of an invitation?*
A. Correct invitations to any wedding, whatever its size, are engraved or thermographed on the first page of a double sheet of heavy paper, ivory or white, either plain or with a raised margin called a plate mark or panel. The invitation may be about 5½ inches wide by 7⅜ inches deep, or slightly smaller, and may be folded once for insertion into its envelope. Or it may be about 4⅜ inches by 5¾ inches and go into the envelope without folding.

When separate invitations to the reception are used, they are engraved on small cards, appropriate to the size chosen for the invitation to the ceremony.

The engraving may be in whatever lettering style the bride and the groom prefer as offered by the stationer, as long as the lettering is clear and easy to read. In general, the simplest styles are in the best taste.

Q. *What is the traditional wording and spelling for a wedding invitation?*
A. There are several traditional rules for wedding invitations:

1. The invitation to the marriage ceremony always reads: " . . . requests the honour [spelled with a "u"] of your presence . . ."
2. The invitation to the reception, when not simply a card saying "Reception following the ceremony," reads " . . . requests the pleasure of your company . . ."
3. No punctuation is used except commas after the day of the week or periods after abbreviations such as "Mr.," "Jr.," St. John's," etc.
4. The date of the wedding is spelled out rather than written as a numeral: "Saturday, the second of September."
5. The time of the wedding is "four o'clock"— never "four P.M." Half hours are written "half after four" or "half past four" rather than "four-thirty." The hour given is the time at which the actual ceremony begins.
6. No words are capitalized except those that

would be ordinarily—people's names and titles, place names, names of day and month.

7. "Doctor" is written in full, unless the name to follow is very long. "Mr." is never written "Mister," but "Jr." may also be written as "Junior," although the abbreviation is preferred.

8. Invitations to Roman Catholic weddings may replace the phrase "at the marriage of" with "at the marriage in Christ of"; "and your participation in the Nuptial Mass" may be added below the groom's name.

9. The address of the church is not included if it is in a small town or city. In larger cities, where not everyone may be acquainted with the whole area, it should be included. If a long street number is included, numerals may be used: "1375 Johnson Lane." If the street name is a numbered street, then spell out the street name: "1559 East Eightieth Street."

10. The year is not included on wedding invitations but usually is on announcements, since in some circumstances they are sent long after the wedding takes place.

11. If the invitation includes the handwritten name of the recipient, the full name must be written out. The use of an initial—"Mr. and Mrs. Robert S. Roth"—is not correct.

12. The invitation to the wedding ceremony alone does not include an R.s.v.p.

13. On the reception invitation "R.S.V.P.,"
"R.s.v.p.," and "The favour of a reply is requested" are all equally correct. If the address
to which the reply is to be sent is different from
that which appears in the invitation itself, you
may use "Kindly send reply to," followed by
the correct address.

The traditional wedding invitation is issued by the bride's parents. Note that although
the bride's name is not preceeded by "Miss,"
the groom's is preceeded by "Mr."

Mr. and Mrs. James Curran Williams
request the honour of your presence
at the marriage of their daughter
Catherine Leigh
to
Mr. Harley Comstock
on Saturday, the twenty-ninth of December
nineteen hundred and ninety
at eleven o'clock
Grace Methodist Church
358 Cornell Drive
Dayton, Ohio

Q. *What is the correct form for an invitation to the
wedding ceremony only?*
A. When a guest is expected to attend the church
service only, the invitation to the reception is not

enclosed. The following wording is correct for all weddings:

Mr. and Mrs. Norbert Rudell
request the honour of your presence
at the marriage of their daughter
Jeanine Marie
to
Mr. Brian Michael Maday
Saturday, the twelfth of April
at half after four o'clock
Church of the Holy Redeemer
Colorado Springs

Q. *Our guest list for the ceremony is larger than for the reception. Do we need a separate invitation to the reception?*

A. Yes, you do. In this case, everyone receives the invitation to the ceremony, and a separate invitation is enclosed for those who are to be invited to the reception. The reception invitation is usually engraved on a card to match the paper and engraving of the church invitation. If the latter is folded for the envelope, then the card is a little smaller than half the full size of the invitation. If it is to go with the smaller invitation that does not fold, it may be from 2½ to 3 inches high by 3½ to 4 inches wide. The most commonly used form is this:

Reception
immediately following the ceremony
Willowridge Country Club
East Lansing
The favour of a reply is requested
112 Chesterfield Parkway
East Lansing, MI 44848

This traditionally worded invitation is correct for all weddings regardless of size. The invitation to a reception following the church ceremony is usually engraved on a card to match the paper and engraving of the church invitation.

Mr. and Mrs Wilson Jennings
request the honour of your presence
at the marriage of their daughter
Joy
to Mr. Richard Kenilworth
Saturday, the eleventh of February
nineteen hundred and ninety
at twelve o'clock
First Evangelist Church
Butte, Montana
R.s.v.p.

Reception
immediately following the ceremony
Church Parish Hall

Q. *What is the correct form for a single invitation to both the wedding ceremony and the reception?*
A. When every guest is invited to both ceremony and reception, the invitation to the reception is included in the invitation to the ceremony. A common form is:

> *Mr. and Mrs. Timothy Clark*
> *request the honour of your presence*
> *at the marriage of their daughter*
> *Amanda Jean*
> *to*
> *Mr. Nelson Finch, Junior*
> *Saturday, the fifteenth of May*
> *at half after three o'clock*
> *Holy Trinity Church*
> *New Rochelle, New York*
> *and afterwards at the reception*
> *123 Mendota Avenue*

R.s.v.p.

Q. *How should a wedding invitation be worded when . . .*
. . . the groom's family gives the wedding?
A. When the invitation is sent in the name of the groom's family, the following form may be used:

Mr. and Mrs. Kenneth Henry Knowles
request the honour of your presence
at the marriage of
Miss Jessica Thorn
to
their son
William Kenneth Knowles
etc.

In this case, the title "Miss" is used, although it is not used otherwise on invitations, with a few exceptions.

Q. ... . *the groom's family is co-hosting the wedding?*
A. The wording would be:

Mr. and Mrs. Nicholas van Reesema
and
Mr. and Mrs. Charles Saunders
request the pleasure of your company
at the wedding reception of
Pamela van Reesema
and
Constantin Saunders
etc.

A separate invitation to the wedding ceremony should be sent in the name of the bride's parents.

Q. . . . *the bride has only one living parent?*
A. If either the bride's mother or father is deceased, and the living parent is giving the wedding alone, the wording would be:

> *Dr. Thomas Reap*
> *[Mrs. Thomas Reap]*
> *requests the honour of your presence*
> *at the marriage of his [her] daughter*
> *Samantha Elizabeth*
> etc.

This same wording would be used if the bride's parents are divorced and only one of them is giving the wedding.

Q. . . . *the bride has a stepfather?*
A. When the bride's own father is not living and she has a stepfather, or her mother has divorced and remarried and her mother and stepfather are responsible for the wedding, the wording would be:

> *Mr. and Mrs. Alexander Thomas Murphy*
> *request the honour of your presence*
> *at the marriage of her daughter*
> *[or their daughter]*
> *Dana Kirsten Murphy*
> etc.

Q. . . . *the couple wish to include the name of a deceased parent?*

A. The name of a deceased parent may not be included in the invitation as if it were being issued by him or her, but it may be included if the invitation is sent by the bride and groom, as follows:

Together with their families,
Abigail Susan Heyel,
daughter of Katherine Heyel
and the late John Henry Heyel,
and
Kevin Marcus Moore,
son of Mr. and Mrs. Marcus Andrew Moore,
request the honour of your presence
etc.

Q. . . . *the bride's divorced and remarried parents are giving the wedding together?*

A. When the bride's parents are divorced, the wedding invitations are issued in the name of the parent who pays for and acts as host at the reception. However, in the event that relations are so friendly that they share the expenses and act as co-hosts, both names should appear on the invitation:

Mr. and Mrs. Robert Martin
[the bride's mother and stepfather]
and
Mr. and Mrs. Victor Ferretti
[the bride's father and stepmother]
request the honour of your presence
at the marriage of
Christina Ferretti
to
Mr. Brian Matthiason
etc.

In the rare event that both the bride's and groom's parents are hosting the wedding—and both are divorced—it would be correct for all four sets of names to be on the invitation.

Q. . . . *the bride has no living parents?*
A. There are several choices for a bride who is an orphan. In a few cases, the exception to the rule is practiced and the title "Miss" or "Mrs." is used before the bride's name.

If the wedding is given by friends, the wording is:

Mr. and Mrs. Michael Cook
request the honour of your presence
at the marriage of
Miss Jennifer White
to
Mr. Parker Adam Stevens
etc.

If the bride has adult brothers or sisters, the oldest one customarily sends out her wedding invitations and announcements in his or her name. If another relative has taken the place of a parent, his or her name is used:

Mr. Deane Flood
requests the honour of your presence
at the marriage of his sister
Rebecca Ann
etc.

Mr. and Mrs. George Roy
request the honour of your presence
at the marriage of their niece
Melody Susan Dieters
etc.

When a bride chooses to send out the invitations in her and her groom's name, the wording is:

The honour of your presence
is requested
at the marriage of
Miss Franca Calgi
to
Mr. Benjamin Struthers
etc.

or

Miss Franca Calgi
and
Mr. Benjamin Struthers
request the honour of your presence
at their marriage
etc.

Q. . . . *the couple and their parents are hosting the wedding?*

A. When the invitation to the marriage is to be issued in the name of both sets of parents and the bride and groom, the wording would be:

> *Miss Judith Budding*
> *and*
> *Mr. Frank Badart Kemp*
> *together with their parents*
> *Mr. and Mrs. Arthur Budding*
> *and*
> *Mr. and Mrs. Edward Kemp*
> *request the honour of your presence*
> *at their marriage*
> etc.

Q. . . . *the bride is a young widow or divorcée?*
A. Invitations to the marriage of a young widow or divorcée are sent in the name of her parents, exactly as the invitation to her first wedding may have been, except that her full name—first, maiden, and married—is included instead of just her first name:

> *Mr. and Mrs. David Hillman*
> *request the honour of your presence*
> *at the marriage of their daughter*
> *Marissa Hillman Cox*
> *to*
> etc.

A more mature widow or one whose parents are deceased may send out her own invitations:

*The honour of your presence
is requested
at the marriage of
Mrs. Timothy Scott McCullough
and
etc.*

If the bride is a young divorcée and is sending out her own invitations, she would not use her former husband's first name but would use her own first name—"Mrs. Vanessa McCullough."

Q. . . . *the groom is in the military?*
A. The name of a bridegroom whose rank is below Lieutenant Commander in the Navy or Coast Guard or Major in the Army, Air Force, or Marine Corps is given this way:

*Warren Miller
Ensign, United States Navy*

Officers of those ranks or above have the title on the same line as their names, and the service below:

*Colonel Stephen Bryers
United States Air Force*

Although "j.g." or "junior grade" is usually used with "Lt." in the Navy, the Army title of "Lt." is not usually preceded by "1st" or "2nd."

Reserve officers on active duty use "Army of the United States" or "United States Naval Reserve" below their names.

Titles used to be written out in full, but today it is acceptable to abbreviate, so that "Lieutenant Commander" may be written "Lt. Commander," "Captain" may be written "Capt.," etc.

Noncommissioned officers and enlisted men in the regular forces may use their titles or not, as they prefer. A private might simply have his name engraved:

Joshua David Brown
United States Air Force

A noncommissioned officer might prefer

Dwight Albright Tucker
Corporal, United States Army

High-ranking regular officers who are retired continue to use their titles and include their service on the line below, with "retired" following the service:

William Brighton Free
United States Army, retired

Q. . . . *the bride is in the military?*
A. The name of a bride who is on active duty in the armed forces is written:

marriage of their daughter
Maryanne
Lieutenant, United States Army

Q. *. . . the bride's father is in the military?*
A. When the father of the bride is a member of the armed forces, on active duty, or is a high-ranking retired officer, he uses his title in the ordinary way:

Colonel and Mrs. Albert Withers
request the honour
etc.

If he is a *retired* high-ranking officer, the invitation reads:

Lieutenant Colonel (Ret.) and Mrs. Steven Blum
request the honour
etc.

Q. *I am a medical doctor and my fiancé holds a Ph.D. Do we use our titles on our invitations?*
A. Your title is not used when the invitation is issued by your parents, in which case it would read "their daughter Lisa." It is used when the invitation is issued by you and your groom:

> *The honour of your presence*
> *is requested*
> *at the marriage of*
> *Dr. Lisa Partridge*
> *and*
> *William Spelman*

Holders of academic degrees do not use the "Dr." unless they are always referred to in that way. If this is the case, the wording on an invitation issued by the bride's parents would be:

> *their daughter Lisa*
> *to*
> *Dr. William Spelman*

The title "Dr." would be inserted before the name on an invitation issued by the bride and the groom.

Q. *My fiancé will receive his medical degree in June, and we are getting married in July. Even though he won't officially be a doctor at the time that we order the invitations, should we use his title on the invitations?*
A. Yes, you may use his title, since he will officially be a doctor at the time of your wedding. His name would be written "Doctor Franklin Pierce." This would hold true for any man in a profession in which the title is ordinarily used, such as a dentist, veterinarian, clergyman, or judge.

Q. *My sister and I are planning a double wedding. How do we word the invitation?*

A. The invitation is worded with the older sister's name given first:

> *Mr. and Mrs. Eric Stockmar*
> *request the honour of your presence*
> *at the marriage of their daughters*
> *Linda Ellen*
> *to*
> *Mr. Paul Degenhardt*
> *and*
> *Lonna Elaine*
> *to*
> *Mr. Andrew Romeo*
> *Saturday, the tenth of May*
> *at one o'clock*
> *Trinity Church*

Q. *Our wedding will be held at a friend's home. Are the invitations issued in their names or in my parents' names?*

A. Invitations are issued by the parents of the bride even though the wedding takes place at a house other than their own. The names of the parents at the head of the invitation mean that they are giving the wedding and probably assuming all expenses, but not in their own house:

Mr. and Mrs. Elias Johnston
request the honour of your presence
at the marriage of their daughter
Eleanor
to
Mr. Carlton Klosek
Saturday, the twenty-first of December
at four o'clock
at the residence [*or home*]
of Mr. and Mrs. John Drakewood
124 Kenwood Parkway
Minneapolis, Minnesota

Q. *We are having a private wedding ceremony with only immediate family present, but would still like to have a reception for family and friends. How would invitations to the reception be worded?*

A. In this case, invitations to the ceremony are given orally or by personal note, and invitations to the reception are sent out separately. The size and style of these invitations are exactly the same as those to the wedding itself. The wording is similar to a ceremony invitation:

Mr. and Mrs. Jasper Kramer
request the pleasure of your company
at the wedding reception
of their daughter
Cara Marie
and
Mr. Alfred Welch
Saturday, the ninth of October
at one o'clock
Ridgefield Hunt Club
Ridgefield, Connecticut

R.s.v.p.
231 Archer Place
South Salem, New York 10590

Q. *My husband and I married in Europe three months ago and have just returned home. Our parents have graciously offered to give a wedding reception for us. How would the invitations be worded?*

A. Although the reception is being held to celebrate your marriage, a true "wedding reception" immediately follows the ceremony. Therefore, an invitation for a belated reception omits the word "wedding." The invitations may be formally engraved or, if you prefer to send a less formal invitation, you may write the necessary information on an informal and at the top write "In honor of" you and your husband. Or you may purchase fill-in invitations appropriate for the occasion. If your invitations will be engraved, the wording would be:

Mr. and Mrs. Philip DeBois
request the pleasure of your company
at a reception
in honor of
Mr. and Mrs. Robert Jefferson Higgins
on
etc.

Q. *What is the proper way to respond to a wedding invitation?*
A. The answer to your question depends on the type of invitation you receive and whether it asks for a handwritten response or has a reply card enclosed. Invitations to the marriage ceremony do not necessitate an answer, unless the invitation has arrived in the form of a personal note. In that case it should be answered at once, also by handwritten note.

Replies to informal invitations need not be in the traditional, third-person style since the invitation is not, but they do require a response, which may be a note written on your own informal or notepaper. If the invitation is in a semiformal style where other than traditional wording is used, the answer might be written in the same form. For example, if the invitation reads:

Our joy will be more complete
if you can share in the marriage of our daughter
Patricia Jean
to
Mr. Roderick John Thorne
on Saturday, the twenty-seventh of June
at half after four o'clock
at Christ's Church
Princeton, New Jersey.
We invite you to worship with us, witness
their vows, and join us for a reception at
the Princeton Inn. If you are unable to
attend, we ask your presence in thought
and prayer.
Mr. and Mrs. Jay Barnett
[or Coraleen and Jay Barnett]

R.s.v.p.
6 Birdsong Lane
Princeton, New Jersey 08540

Your response might read:

> *We will be happy*
> *to share your joy*
> *and participate in*
> *the marriage of your daughter*
> *Patricia Jean*
> *on Saturday, the twenty-seventh of June*
> *Margaret and Donald Hewlitt*

The traditional, third-person reply is written exactly in the form of the invitation. This formal reply should be written on plain or bordered, monogrammed or unmarked letter paper or notepaper, in black or blue ink. The lines should be evenly and symmetrically spaced on one page. The wording for an acceptance is:

> *Mr. and Mrs. James Dolce*
> *accept with pleasure*
> *the kind invitation of*
> *Mr. and Mrs. Jay Barnett*
> *for Saturday, the twenty-seventh of June*

or

Mr. and Mrs. James Dolce
accept with pleasure
Mr. and Mrs. Barnett's
kind invitation for
Saturday, the twenty-seventh of June

If regretting the invitation, the wording is:

Mr. and Mrs. James Dolce
regret that they are unable to accept
Mr. and Mrs. Barnett's
kind invitation for
Saturday, the twenty-seventh of June

(Or "the kind invitation of Mr. and Mrs. Jay Barnett for . . .")

If the invitation includes a reply card, it should be filled in and returned instead of a handwritten response.

Q. *Is it in good taste to enclose reply cards with invitations to a wedding reception?*

A. Response cards are used so frequently now that the former breach of etiquette they represented is no longer an issue. They certainly expedite replies, enabling you to know more quickly how many guests to expect, since recipients find it easier to fill in the card than to handwrite a response. If response cards are enclosed with wedding invitations, a self-addressed envelope is included, preferably stamped. It is unwise to put "Number of people" on the card. Even though the envelope is addressed to "Mr. and Mrs. John Smith," when Mr. and Mrs. Smith see that, followed by a blank line, they might think their entire family is invited. The best form for the wedding response card is:

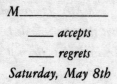

M_____

_____ accepts

_____ regrets

Saturday, May 8th

Because the return envelope is addressed, no address is necessary under the R.s.v.p. on the invitation.

Q. *How can one tell invitees that their children are not included?*
A. Perhaps the best way to indicate to invited guests that their children are not included in the invitation (even when the invitation is not addressed to the children) is to enclose a note with invitations to relatives and close friends who might think their children would be welcome. In the note, explain that children cannot be included, and why. Generally, the "why" has to do with space or cost.

If possible, young children could be invited to the ceremony, and the note could suggest this, indicating that you would love to have them at the ceremony but cannot invite them to the reception. The bride could also speak to friends and relatives, asking them to mention that children cannot be included when they speak to other friends and relatives. It is important, if this is an issue, however, that no exceptions are made, other than the bride's young brothers and sisters and those of the groom.

Q. *My fiancé and I are giving our own wedding. May we still send out the invitations in our parents' names?*
A. Of course you may. More and more brides and grooms today are paying the costs of their weddings, but there is no rule that states that the invitation must reflect this.

Q. *Why aren't the names of the groom's mother and father included on the wedding invitation?*
A. Traditionally, the cost of the wedding reception is that of the bride's family. Because they are, therefore, the hosts, they would issue the invitations. In this case, the groom's parents are honored guests, not hosts, even though their own friends and family are included on the guest list. If, however, the groom's parents are sharing equally in paying the costs, their names may and should be included on the invitation.

Q. *Why are tissues included in wedding invitations?*
A. They are included today primarily because they are traditional. Engravers used to use tissue sheets to protect the pages from the fresh ink. With the improvements in engraving techniques or when thermography is used, tissues are no longer necessary. They may be used, placed on top of the printed surface of the invitation, or they may be omitted.

Q. *I received an invitation with a small card that says "Within the ribbon." What do I do with it?*
A. These cards are for reserved pews. Very often, a white satin ribbon will be extended at the ends of a number of pews to indicate that they are reserved for family and intimate friends. Even if ribbons are not used, the phrase "Within the ribbon" indicates that you are expected to sit near the front. The card you received is called a pew card. You take it with you to the ceremony and show it to the usher so that he knows that a space has been reserved for you.

Q. *What is an at-home card?*
A. When the bride and groom want their friends to know what their address is to be, an at-home card may be included with the invitation. These cards follow this form:

Mr. and Mrs. Baxter will be at home
after the sixth of June
30 East Thirty-seventh Street
New York, New York 10036

An at-home card is approximately 4 inches by 2½ inches, slightly smaller than a reception card.

Q. *Why are there often two envelopes for a wedding invitation?*
A. Tradition is one of the reasons for the use of two envelopes today, going back to the fact that many, many years ago, when invitations were delivered by hand, they were politely left unsealed. Later, when all letters began to be delivered by mail, these same unsealed envelopes were inserted in a larger envelope that could be sealed. The continued use of inner envelopes today is a practical one in that the names of children can be listed on them, which saves sending separate invitations or listing all the names in one family on the outer envelope, which can be confusing. They are not mandatory, however, and if time and budget do not permit their use, they may be omitted.

Q. *When there are two envelopes, how are they addressed?*
A. The proper procedure for an inner envelope is

to address it "Mr. and Mrs. Smythe," with neither first name nor address. When the outer envelope is addressed to "Mr. and Mrs. Kent Smythe and family," the inner envelope is addressed:

Mr. and Mrs. Smythe
Jules, Karen, and Barbara

When children receive their own invitations, the outer envelope is addressed to "The Misses Karen and Barbara Smythe and Messr. Jules Smythe," and the inner envelope reads "Karen, Barbara, and Jules." Inner envelopes to close relatives may be addressed "Grandmother," "Aunt Ruth and Uncle Don," etc. The way to tell the difference between the inner and the outer envelopes is that the former have no mucilage, since they are not to be sealed, and, of course, they are smaller.

Outer envelopes are addressed like any other mailing envelope, with certain exceptions. No abbreviations should be used, either in the name of the addressee or the address. "Street," "Avenue," and the state name are all written out in full. The middle name of the recipient may be omitted, but if it is used, it too should be written out. Only if the name is exceptionally long might an initial be used. Children's names are written below their parents' if the phrase "and family" is not used.

Q. *How is the inner envelope inserted into the mailing envelope?*

A. Hold the stuffed inner envelope with the unsealed flap at the top and facing away from you. Insert it into the outer, or mailing, envelope so that when the outer envelope is opened, "Mr. and Mrs. Smythe" is facing the flap side. Seal the mailing envelope.

The order for placing the invitation and any cards into the inner envelope is as follows: A folded invitation designed to fit an envelope half its size will require a second fold, which should be made with the engraving folded to the inside. All insertions (such as a reception card, a response card, an at-home card, or a pew card) are placed inside the second fold, with the type facing the flap of the envelope. Insert the filled, folded invitation, folded edge first, into the inner envelope.

If the invitation is not folded a second time, the cards are inserted in front of it (nearest you), with the reception card next to the invitation and any smaller cards in front of that. If tissue is used in either case, it is placed over the type of the invitation so that the cards are placed on top of the tissue.

Q. *My fiancé and I find traditional wedding invitations too formal for our tastes. Can we write our own invitations? If so, can you suggest the wording?*

A. Yes, you may write your own invitations, as

long as they are dignified, attractive, and sincerely reflect the sentiments of the bride, the groom, and their families. Following is a very simple example, written in the bride's hand:

Lee Spencer and Peter Davis

invite you to
celebrate their
marriage

on
Saturday, September
the eighth
at four o'clock

44 Beach Road, Essex, Connecticut

R S.V.P.

Another, from the bride's parents, is on page 117. It might be sent for a semitraditional formal wedding. There are many other possibilities, and prospective brides and grooms should explore them, keeping in mind that the invitations should be appropriate to the other plans for the wedding.

Q. *We are inviting only twenty people to our wedding. Would it be proper to send handwritten notes rather than printed invitations?*
A. Yes, a note written personally by the bride is a most flattering invitation. For example:

Dear Aunt Amanda,

  Charles and I are to be married at Holy Trinity Church at half past one on Friday, the tenth. We hope you and Uncle Richard will come to the church and afterward to the reception at Shenorock Shore Club.

  With much love from us both,
  Affectionately,
  Brenda

This type of note may also be sent in lieu of an engraved invitation to guests who are very special to the bride or groom for a larger wedding and when the wedding is held on short notice. In the latter circumstance, telephone invitations are also perfectly correct.

Q. *Just when may an invitation be addressed to "Mr. and Mrs. John Smith and family"?*
A. Envelopes are addressed this way when everyone in the household receiving the invitation is invited to the wedding. They may not be addressed this way if only one of three children is invited, for example, or if none of the children is invited. This form of address is fine when there is an inner envelope so that the names of the children may be written individually. If only an outer envelope is used, however, it is preferable to address it "Mr. and Mrs. John Smith" on the first line, "Miss Carolyn Smith" on the second, and "Messr. Daniel Smith"

on the third so that it is very clear exactly who is
being invited.

Q. *Is the zip code ever included in the body of the
invitation?*
A. Only when the address to which replies are to
be sent does not appear on the envelope or following the R.s.v.p. on the invitation would the zip code
be included in the body of the invitation.

Q. *At what age should children receive their own invitations?*
A. Boys and girls over the age of twelve or thirteen
should, when possible, be sent their own invitations.

Q. *Should wedding invitations have return addresses
on the envelope?*
A. Yes they should, and there are three good reasons for this. First, the United States Postal Service
requests that all first-class mail carry a return address. Second, the inclusion of a return address provides invited guests with a definite address to which
to send a reply and a gift. And third, the return
address ensures that the bride will know if the invitation did not reach the destination, since it would
be returned to her for a correct address.

In the past it was considered to be in poor taste
to put the return address on a wedding invitation
envelope but, for the reasons given above, I believe
it is time to change this guideline, and I firmly

recommend that a legible return address be engraved on the back flap of the envelope or written in the front upper-left corner.

Q. *Should invitations be sent to . . .*
. . . the person who performs the ceremony and his or her spouse?
A. Yes, the clergyperson who performs the ceremony and his or her spouse should be sent an invitation to the reception. They may choose not to attend if they are not acquainted with one family or the other, but it would be discourteous not to include them on the list. Unless he or she is a personal friend, the clergyperson is not obligated to send a gift.

Q. *. . . the fiancé(e) of an invited guest?*
A. When a bride knows that an invited guest or a member of her wedding party is engaged, she should, whether she knows the fiancé(e) or not, send him (or her) a separate invitation. If she does not know the name and cannot find out, she may write "and guest" on the inner envelope or write on the invitation, "We would be delighted to have you bring your fiancé(e)." This same guideline is true when the bride knows that a friend is living with someone but does not know his or her name. In either case, it is preferable to try to determine the name of the unknown person, since it makes him or her feel more welcome to receive his or her own

invitation, or to be included by name on the inner envelope.

Q. . . . *the bridal party members?*
A. Yes, they are sent invitations as mementos, but it is not expected that they will respond, except in the case of another guest being included in their invitation, in which case you need to know whether the guest will be attending.

Q. . . . *the groom's parents?*
A. Yes, because the invitation serves as a memento for them. Again, they need not acknowledge the invitation unless they have had no contact with the bride's family.

Q. . . . *small children who are not invited to the reception?*
A. Youngsters who cannot be included at the reception are often delighted with an invitation to the church ceremony. Their parents may not be as delighted, however, if arrangements for transporting them back home while their parents go on to the reception are difficult. If possible, call the parents and explain that, although you are not able to invite their children to the reception, you would very much like to have them attend the ceremony. If you are sending separate invitations to the ceremony, ask them if it would be all right to send their children one, or if it would set up disappointment and they would prefer that you did not.

Q. . . . *people in mourning?*
A. Yes. It is not your decision whether they will feel like attending. If you would have included them were they not in mourning, you should still include them at this time, with the decision to attend or not left to them.

Q. . . . *one member of a married couple and not his or her spouse?*
A. No. It is obligatory that you invite both, even when you do not know one of them or when you do not like one of them. In responding, it is all right for one to attend without the other, but both must be invited.

Q. *May I invite only one member of an unmarried couple who are living together?*
A. No, an unmarried couple living together is considered the same as a married couple, and both persons must be invited. Their names are written on two separate lines on one invitation envelope.

Q. *Is it proper to invite co-workers in your office to your wedding with a single invitation posted on the bulletin board?*
A. You may do this, but only if every person in the office is included. One of your wedding invitations, open, should be posted, with "To Members of the Staff" written at the top. Since there is no envelope addressed to "Mr. and Mrs." or to "Miss Jones and fiancé," a note must be placed beside the invitation

stating that husbands and wives (and fiancés, fiancées, and dates if you wish) are invited as well. To ensure that co-workers know that you really hope they will come, and also so you will know how many to plan for, post a paper headed "If you are able to come, please sign here, and indicate whether your husband, wife, date, or escort will be with you."

Q. *We've changed the date of our wedding. Our invitations have already been printed. Can we cross out the old date and insert the new one?*
A. Yes, you may, since to reprint the invitations would involve an enormous, duplicate expense. Be sure to be as neat as is possible. If time and budget permit, you may instead enclose a small printed card saying "The date of the wedding has been changed from . . . to. . . ." If the number of guests is small, a small card with the same information may be written by hand and enclosed with the printed invitation.

Q. *We canceled our wedding plans shortly after mailing the invitations. How do we inform people?*
A. When wedding plans are postponed indefinitely after the invitations have been mailed, it is necessary to send the news out as soon as possible. If it is possible to have cards printed in time, they are the best solution for informing people. The wording, depending on the reason for the cancellation, would be:

Owing to the sudden death of
Mr. Thomas Ilse
the marriage of his daughter
Georgia
to
Mr. Nicholas Jennings
has been postponed

or

Mr. and Mrs. Peter Vandermuellen
regret that
due to the groom's immediate transfer to Malta
the date of
Susan Vandermuellen's wedding
to Mr. Chad Bridges
must be indefinitely postponed

When the wedding is definitely canceled and will not take place, printed cards should be sent which read:

Mr. and Mrs. Bradley Allesso
announce that the marriage of their daughter
Pamela Lynn
to
Mr. Paul Staley
will not take place

If gifts have already been received, they must be returned. If the cancellation is an indefinite post-ponement but the couple intend to be married as soon as possible, the gifts are carefully put away until the time the ceremony takes place. If there is doubt whether it will take place at all, the gifts must be returned after six to eight weeks so that the donors may return them to the store. A note like the following should be enclosed.

> *Dear Jeanette,*
>
> *I am sorry to have to tell you that Chad and I have canceled our wedding plans.*
>
> *Therefore I am returning the tea service that you were so sweet to send me.*
>
> *Love,*
> *Susan*

Q. *How do announcements differ from invitations? Who gets them and who doesn't?*
A. Wedding announcements serve to announce that a wedding has taken place and are sent after the wedding, either the same day or the day after, although they may be sent out up to a year later. It is never obligatory to send announcements, but they do serve a useful purpose. Since they carry no obligation that the recipient send a gift in return, they are far more practical than invitations when sent to people who would like to know about the

wedding, but who are not close enough to be expected to send a present. They may also be sent to old friends who have been out of touch with the bride's or groom's family for a long time; business associates, clients, etc.; people who live too far away to be able to attend the wedding; and to close friends who cannot be included if the wedding and reception lists are limited. Announcements are not sent to those who receive invitations.

Q. *How is an announcement worded?*
A. The form of the wedding announcement resembles the form of the wedding invitation in almost everything except wording. Announcements have traditionally been sent in the name of the bride's parents, but in spite of this traditional "rule," I feel, and recommend, that the family of the groom be included on the announcement with that of the bride. Today the attitude toward marriage is one of joining, rather than giving the bride to the groom, and furthermore, the purpose of an announcement, unlike an invitation, is to give as much information as possible. Surely the groom's parents are an important part of the pertinent information! The inclusion of their names is not only informative but also indicates their approval and joy in the marriage. Therefore, while the traditional wording is as follows,

Mr. and Mrs. Samuel Harding
have the honour of
announcing the marriage of their daughter
Mary Ellen
to
Mr. Vincent Parsons
Saturday, the fifth of August
One thousand nine hundred and ninety
Our Savior Church
Des Moines, Iowa

I prefer, when agreed upon and appropriate,

Mr. and Mrs. Samuel Harding
and
Mr. and Mrs. Frederick Parsons
announce the marriage of
Mary Ellen Harding
and
Vincent Bruce Parsons
Saturday, the fifth of August
One thousand nine hundred and ninety
Our Savior Church
Des Moines, Iowa

Note that while most wedding invitations use the phrase "the marriage of their daughter . . . to

. . . ," the announcement often reads "the marriage of . . . and. . . ."

Since "Mary Ellen Harding" is not preceded by "Miss" in the second example above, neither should "Vincent Bruce Parsons" be preceded by "Mr." When "to" is used in place of "and," however, the "Mr." is used, just as it is on a wedding invitation.

Three forms of phrasing are equally correct: "have the honour to announce"; "have the honour of announcing"; or simply the one word "announce." The variations in wording necessitated by special circumstances—such as stepparents, a widowed parent, etc.—correspond to the variations in wedding invitations.

Mr. and Mrs. Hamilton Plunkett
and
Mr. and Mrs. Carleton Ferris
announce the marriage of
Diane Marie Plunkett
and William Lee Ferris
Thursday, the seventeenth of May
Mormon Tabernacle Church
Salt Lake City, Utah

Q. *My daughter was widowed and will soon be wed again. How would her announcement read?*
A. Her announcement would include her present

full name, as would an announcement for a young divorcée who has retained her ex-husband's name:

> *Mr. and Mrs. Ard Farrington*
> *announce the marriage of their daughter*
> *Brooke Farrington Hough*
> etc.

The announcement of the second marriage of a mature widow or divorcée reads differently:

> *Mrs. William Philip Hoyt*
> *and*
> *Mr. Worthington Adams*
> *announce their marriage*
> *on Monday, the second of November*
> etc.

Q. *My parents are opposed to my marriage, so my fiancé and I are giving our own wedding. May we send announcements in our name, or do they have to be in my parents' name?*
A. You may send your announcements in your own names, as may a bride who has no parents or other relatives who might otherwise issue the announcements. Your announcement would read:

Miss Kimberly Williams
and
Mr. Scott Adam Schiffer
announce their marriage
on Saturday, the sixth of February
etc.

Q. *My fiancé and I, who are both in our 30's, have been living together for quite some time. Although we are having a small, traditional wedding which we are giving ourselves, we would like to send announcements to friends and relatives who will not be invited. Our relationships with our parents are close, but it seems silly to have the announcements in their name just for proper form. Is this necessary?*

A. No, it is not necessary. If it would please you and your parents to have the announcements sent in their name, you may of course have them printed that way. Otherwise, they may be sent from you and your groom, in your names.

Your invitations and announcements may read:

Pamela Cynthia Marston
and
Dennis Lawrence Pearson
invite you to share with them
the joy of their marriage
Saturday, the nineteenth of March
nineteen hundred and ninety
at half after five o'clock
First Baptist Church
Atlanta, Georgia

Pamela Cynthia Marston
and
Dennis Lawrence Pearson
announce their marriage
on Saturday, the nineteenth of March
nineteen hundred and ninety
Atlanta, Georgia

Q. *My parents are deceased and my aunt and uncle are giving our wedding. May they send announcements in their name?*

A. Yes, they may. The wording is optional and may indicate their relationship to you or simply show your name:

Mr. and Mrs. Frederick Roberts
announce the marriage of
Miss Judith Espinar
(or, their niece, Miss Judith Espinar)
etc.

Q. *Our future daughter-in-law has been estranged from her parents for years and my husband and I are giving te wedding. We would like to send announcements to those friends who will not be invited to the wedding. Is it corrects for them to be issued in our name?!*

A. Certainly. The wording would be:

Mr. and Mrs. James Carvelas
announce the marriage of
Miss Catherine Elizabeth Walsh
and Mr. Louis James Carvelas
etc.

Index

About the Author

Elizabeth L. Post, granddaughter-in-law of the legendary Emily Post, has earned the mantle of her predecessor as America's foremost authority on etiquette. Mrs. Post has revised the classic *Etiquette* four times since 1965, and has written *Emily Post's Complete Book of Wedding Etiquette*; *Emily Post's Wedding Planner*; *Please, Say Please*; *The Complete Book of Entertaining* with co-author Anthony Staffieri; *Emily Post Talks with Teens* with co-author Joan M. Coles; along with other titles in this series of question-and-answer books: *Emily Post on Etiquette*, *Emily Post on Entertaining*, *Emily Post on Weddings,* and *Emily Post on Business Etiquette*. Mrs. Post's advice on etiquette may also be found in the monthly column she writes for *Good Housekeeping* magazine, "Etiquette for Every Day."

Mrs. Post and her husband divide their time between homes in Florida and Vermont.